MW00490428

We Would Be One

We Would Be One

A History of
Unitarian Universalist Youth Movements

Wayne Arnason and Rebecca Scott

SKINNER HOUSE BOOKS

BOSTON

Copyright © 2005 by the Unitarian Universalist Association. Published by Skinner House Books. Skinner House Books is an imprint of the Unitarian Universalist Association, a liberal religious organization with more than 1,000 congregations in the U.S. and Canada. 25 Beacon St., Boston, MA 02108.

Printed in the United States.

Cover design by Bruce Jones.

ISBN 1-55896-488-6

Library of Congress Cataloging-in-Publication Data

Arnason, Wayne B. (Wayne Bergthor), 1950-
  We would be one : a history of Unitarian Universalist youth movements / Wayne Arnason and Rebecca Scott.
     p. cm.
  Includes bibliographical references and index.
  ISBN 1-55896-488-6 (alk. paper)
1. Church group work with youth—Unitarian Universalist Association—History. 2. Unitarian Universalist Association—History. 3. Youth movement—United States—History. I. Scott, Rebecca, 1969- II. Title.

BX9856.A76 2005
267'.629132--dc22

                                                                    2004030650

  5 4 3 2 1
08 07 06 05

"Follow the Gleam" by Helen Hill Miller, YWCA, 1923. Reprinted by permission of the YWCA.

Contents

Foreword

WAYNE ARNASON AND REBECCA SCOTT have done a wonderful piece of work in revising and updating the story of our ministry to and with youth. The weaving together of the facts with the personal stories and testimonials of those who were involved, both as youth and as adults, highlights the themes that are a part of youth ministry. The stories are critical because youth ministry, like any ministry, is personal.

The various institutional structures, the several names we have called them, the ways our faith has found to bring youth and adults into partnership, the decisions of youth leadership, the UUA Board, and indeed the influence of past UUA presidents, are the traditional "facts" of a history. But this book recounts far more. It is the history of faith community leaders of all ages struggling to find a way to minister effectively to and with persons who are living through the difficult transition from youth to adulthood.

And my own story is a part of this history. In 1961, at the age of fourteen, I found Unitarian Universalism at First Unitarian Church in Cincinnati, Ohio. But more importantly, I found Liberal Religious Youth (LRY). LRY rapidly became my church. It offered opportunities for leadership, empowered me, and offered me a place where I "fit," something I seemed unable to find anywhere else. I do not mean to imply that LRY (and the YRUU structure that followed it) were or are only places for misfit youth. But one of the developmental tasks of youth is to find where you belong. That means experimentation and often critique of existing structures.

As a sophomore at Harvard, I became president of Continental LRY. My executive committee of seven members included three people of color. We assumed that Unitarian Universalism would soon come to look like our youth programs. How bitterly disappointed we were. I also remember that the perennial behavioral issue of sexual experimentation was beginning to be eclipsed by questions of drug use.

In 1993 my son Billy discovered Young Religious Unitarian Universalists (YRUU) at First Unitarian Church in Oakland, California. Now in the role of parent, I often took him and his friends to YRUU "Cons." Though they now regularly featured blue and pink hair and piercings, the Cons seemed very much like the LRY conferences of my youth. YRUU worked for my son. It fit him.

I joined the UUA staff in 1994 and consulted with district after district dealing with violations of behavioral covenants at YRUU gatherings, trying each time to remember the issues of my years in LRY leadership.

I remember UUA moderator Denny Davidoff calling me one day in 2001 to ask me, "Do you know where your son is?" "He's sitting with the UUA Board helping us understand the need for youth presence at the Board table," she told me. Empowerment at work.

My daughter Danielle did not join YRUU in her high school years. YRUU, like LRY before it, has a distinct culture. She seemed to "fit" better in her school environment.

At my first meeting with the YRUU Steering Committee as president of the UUA in 2001, they asked me to discuss what *youth empowerment* meant to me and how I planned to support it. I responded with an affirmation, but it was an affirmation lived out in the partnership between youth and adults. I did not want YRUU to mistake youth empowerment for adult abandonment.

The themes of our youth ministry are perennial. Even as our national culture shifts and different specific issues come to the fore, the developmental tasks of youth remain the same and therefore so do many of the challenges of ministry to and with youth.

We are a religious community and what we do is to offer one another ministry. We hope that the ministry we do together is both healing and empowering, especially our ministry with young people, whose central developmental task is the finding of their own power and responsibility.

In the pages of this book you will find testimonials and stories of former Unitarian Universalist youth leaders who are now denominational leaders. These stories bring to life the excitement of youth, the sense of hope and possibility, the courage to question what is and to imagine what could be. I cherish these stories.

But we know that many of our youth do not maintain contact with our faith, do not find a nurturing spiritual home in our congregations. Is that a failure of our structures? Do we accept it as a given that many of our youth will wander in the wilderness before returning to the fold—if they return at all?

I know that we need to find ways to more adequately support our youth (and our young adult) ministry. As I write in March 2005, a process is beginning to re-imagine our ministry to and with youth. We begin again, hoping to find more opportunities for youth to "fit" in our beloved faith.

As Wayne and Rebecca write in their conclusion, "The only thing we can count on for the future is that Unitarian Universalist youth will continually reinvent the wheel." The publication of this book comes at a good time. My hope is that making more of our history of youth ministry available will inform and deepen our new process for change.

Rev. William Sinkford, President
Unitarian Universalist Association of Congregations
May 2005

Introduction

THE STORY OF THE Unitarian Universalist youth movements is a story about a family coming to terms with its children in the awkward and exciting time between childhood and adulthood. Like any such story, it reflects the tensions between responsibility and freedom, individuality and belonging, comfort and growth. The central themes running through these stories are independence and interdependence. These themes have more often been defined by slogans like "youth autonomy." Youth autonomy has been a focus of engaged debate in Unitarian Universalist youth work for longer than might be expected. In the 1924 "youth issue" of *The Universalist Leader*, Stanley Manning, director of "young people's work" within the Universalist Convention, wrote,

> The first joy to be found in such a position is the discovery that no one can be a director of young people's work. There is so much of initiative, of willingness to work, of desire to explore and discover on their part that no one can direct their activities…This does not mean that there is not an entire willingness to discuss method and ways of working, that there is no desire for advice and assistance; but the very genius of young people's work lies in its self-direction.

Writing almost forty years later, in 1963, Liberal Religious Youth (LRY) president Maria Fleming reflected,

We depend on adults for their counsel in the functioning of our organizations; we need their experience and knowledge as we set up programs, conduct workshops, and write pamphlets; we depend on advisors to chaperone our functions so we can hold these functions; we depend on the financial support of the denomination for the very existence of continental Liberal Religious Youth. And yet, we do have some meaning in mind when we talk about youth autonomy now; we mean basically the right for youth to determine their own programs. This means that we think no one knows better what young people are interested in than young people themselves.

The ideals expressed by these two leaders sound the same, but in context they had come to mean very different things over the years. The phrase "youth autonomy" was not widely used until after 1947, but in a sense, youth organizations of the 1930s enjoyed more real independence than their more recent counterparts, LRY and Young Religious Unitarian Universalists (YRUU), ever have. Stanley Manning described the *capability* of young people to run their programs on their own. Maria Fleming argued for the *right to self-determination* above and beyond the ability of young people to carry out programs entirely unaided. In recent years, discussions within YRUU and the UUA about youth autonomy have been profoundly influenced by anti-racist, anti-oppression, and multicultural education and commitments within both organizations. Since the scope of this history extends only to 2000, these recent learnings and conversations are not reflected in this book.

Two goals of this book are to explore both the continuities and discontinuities flowing through the diverse names, forms, and cultures of Unitarian Universalism's youth organizations. Finding the continuities is particularly important because local youth groups and youth advisors have relatively short careers together. A "generation" of high-school-age people is as short as three years in a local congregation. Volunteer advisors seldom remain longer in such settings. At the district and continental levels, leaders often lack access to records that would give them an overview of the past. Changes in age ranges and in cultural styles can lead one to believe at first glance that youth movements fifty or one hundred years apart have little in common.

Some continuities stand out, however, as particularly important. The election of Rev. Bill Sinkford as president of the Unitarian Universalist Association in 2001 reminded us how often notable leaders in our movement begin their leadership careers through our youth movements; John Haynes Holmes, Frederick May Eliot, Roger Etz, Dorothy Tilden Spoerl, Dana McLean Greeley, Max Kapp, Gordon McKeeman, Peter Raible, Leon Hopper, Larry Ladd, and Robert Eller-Isaacs are just a few examples.

The history of our youth movement is inextricably tied to that of Unitarian Universalism itself. The most significant example is the merger between the Unitarian and Universalist youth movements that created Liberal Religious Youth in 1953, a journey into uncharted waters that anticipated some of the conflicts between Unitarian and Universalist styles and personalities that would emerge in the denominational merger eight years later.

This history will have particular meaning for several different UU communities. Perhaps you are a religious educator: Adolescence is among life's most crucial periods for faith development, and this history may help you understand the most pressing spiritual needs and questions of young people and how you can best serve them. Perhaps you have a particular interest in church history or in voluntary associations: We believe that the stories of the Unitarian Universalist youth movement teach us about both the persistent patterns and sudden shifts in cultural values that have shaped the course of all twentieth-century institutions. Perhaps you yourself are part of this history, or perhaps you are now a youth movement participant, advisor, or seminarian who wonders about the forces that shaped our current youth program. This book is for all of you. We believe it's vital to know where we've been, to tell the stories, to notice where and why we changed, and to remember those who were involved.

Speaking personally, one exciting aspect of preparing this updated history—an expansion of the story first told in *Follow the Gleam*—is that we both participated in some of the events it chronicles. Wayne Arnason held a leadership role during a controversial period of Liberal Religious Youth (LRY) history from 1968 to 1970, and eventually became the Unitarian Universalist Association's director of youth programs from 1980 to 1984 during the process that created Young Religious Unitarian Universalists (YRUU). Rebecca Scott was a youth programs specialist in the UUA's Youth Office from 1989 to 1990 and has written about a stage of YRUU history that coincides with her personal involvement in that organization.

As players in this story, we are acutely aware that the most important meanings of the Unitarian Universalist youth movements lie between the cracks of this institutional history. These meanings are to be found in the oral histories, the shared memories, and the new meanings that zip back and forth across the Internet every day. The personal memoirs between the chapters are offered to help convey those meanings. Inevitably, even these remembrances will fall short of capturing how important UU youth groups, conferences, and organizations have been in peoples' lives for over a century. What has made the alphabet soup of YPCU, YPRU, AUY, UYF, LRY, SRL, IRF, YRUU, and C*UUYAN such a nourishing broth has been the "people soup" of relationships—relationships of depth, quality, and duration that been formed at crucial times in individual lives and have often grown across lifetimes.

Occasionally the stories of these relationships are glimpsed in this institutional narrative: stories of adventure, fear, risk, and love. They are stories of when and how we knew we were growing up, and what that meant to us. They are the stories of how religious education evolves as we do grow up, and how religious education turns into faith development that lasts a lifetime.

Laying the Foundations

THE YOUTH MOVEMENTS of the Universalist and Unitarian churches had their beginnings in a larger groundswell of "youth" activity across the denominational spectrum in the late nineteenth century. This, in turn, was one aspect of a more general movement of voluntary organizations within churches that produced women's groups, altar guilds, and men's clubs.

By that time, both the Universalist and Unitarian churches had long-standing Sunday School societies, Sunday School programs devised by denominational committees or local churches included material for "senior" grades (today's high school age). However, there was no specific young people's organization on any national or continental level. It appears that already in American institutional religion, the period between ages fourteen and thirty had been identified as a time of both problem and potential, an explosive time loaded with energy that needed channeling. Dwight L. Moody, the famous evangelist, had perceived the potential of a student religious movement as early as 1866 when he organized the Student Volunteer Movement for Christian Missions.

The Unitarians and Universalists had launched no such specific efforts. Jenkin Lloyd Jones, the renowned missionary secretary of the Western Unitarian Conference, began what he called a Mutual Improvement Club in 1874 in his church in Janesville, Wisconsin. It was to be "a combination of post-graduate Sunday

School study, adult education, and social-service and reform work."

The idea caught on in the Western Unitarian Conference. By 1882 there were thirty groups known as "Unity Clubs." Their largely literary and philosophical programs were well attended by people under the age of thirty-five. However, these were not "young people's groups" in the sense that we would use that term today. High-school-age people were not involved in them.

The event that initiated the proliferation of church groups specifically intended for young people occurred in the Williston Congregational Church in Portland, Maine. There, Rev. F. E. Clark founded a Young People's Society for Christian Endeavor (YPSCE). Clark's idea spread beyond the Congregational denomination. Between 1881 and 1889, some thirty-eight Christian Endeavor Societies were founded in Universalist Churches.

The Lynn Convention

The Universalist General Convention (UGC) attempted as early as 1884 to organize these groups into a single Universalist youth organization. In 1886, the UGC Committee on Mission Boxes proposed a plan to create a unified Young People's Missionary Society (YPMS) with branches in every church. The response was not overwhelming. Though fifty-five of these Missionary Society groups had been brought into the fold or created by 1889, numerous Universalist young people's groups remained unaffiliated with any larger body.

The potential for a unified youth movement was there, however. In 1883, some young ministers in Western New York launched a newspaper for Universalist young people entitled *The Universalist Union*. Shortly afterward, one of its publishers, Rev. Stephen Herbert Roblin answered a call to a church in Bay City, Michigan, where he organized a highly successful YPSCE group. He and two other members of the group, Albert C. Grier and Alfred J. Cardell, were particularly interested in propagating the idea of a national union. Together they initiated a letter to all Universalist young people's societies calling for a national organization of Universalist young people.

The reaction was mixed. In 1899, Mr. Grier wrote,

> There followed dark days. Replies poured in and at times I dreaded to open my mail. Discouragements of all sorts came upon us. But few had any such society. Some have YPMS's and were extremely jealous of anything that was to discipline them; others had literary societies and wanted nothing more; others yet thought that such a society had no business in our church; it was bringing in unorthodox methods and would teach young people cant and hypocrisy.

The suggestion met with concern within the Universalist General Convention as well. UGC leaders worried about a competitor for the loyalty of their young people and delegated one UGC executive to sit in on and monitor the first conference of the organizing committee.

In 1889, the Universalist General Convention held its General Assembly in Lynn, Massachusetts. The Lynn church had a strong young people's group, which supported the idea of a union. In conjunction with the young people from Michigan, this group organized a convention of young people on the day preceding the meeting of the UGC.

One hundred and thirty-one delegates representing fifty-six societies from thirteen states attended. On October 22, 1889, they hammered out a constitution, and, after some controversy, chose to call themselves "The Young People's Christian Union of the Universalist Church." In a 1937 letter, delegate Walter Stuart Kelley recalled the debate over the name:

> The most discussion developed over the name, with the contention that the word "Universalist" should be used: either Young People's Universalist Union (or Society) or Universalist Young People's Union. My argument for the name on the constitution as drafted was based upon two points: first, there

was a good deal of misconception among orthodox people as to the religious state of the Universalist, and for that reason we should declare ourselves Christian; and second, the young people of the Congregational Church, in organizing the Christian Endeavor Society, had not seen fit to give it a denominational limitation, and I considered it a good precedent to follow. I made the concession of adding for ourselves "of the Universalist Church" and with this the name was adopted by the Committee and by the convention.

A Bay City man, Lee E. Joslyn, was elected first president of the Union, with James O. Tillinghast of Buffalo, New York, becoming secretary and Nannie Jemison of Lynn, Massachusetts, treasurer. *The Universalist Union* became the official publication.

Thus the Young People's Christian Union (YPCU) of the Universalist Church became the first self-initiated, specifically denominational youth organization (despite Kelley's attraction to the Congregational example). The YPCU preceded and set an example for the Unitarians as well as for the Baptists, Lutherans, and Methodists, who all followed suit within the next decade.

The Young People's Religious Union and the Young People's Christian Union

Prior to 1896, three different groups within the American Unitarian Association (AUA) had competed for members among young adults. One was the National Bureau of Unity Clubs, led by the well-known Unitarian leader Edward Everett Hale as president. The National Bureau encouraged communication between the groups and sponsored special events and lectures featuring Boston luminaries such as Julia Ward Howe. In addition to his Unity Club work, Hale originated the "Lend-A-Hand Clubs," which mingled social activity with philanthropic projects.

In 1887, a movement of "young people's guilds" began in a Unitarian society in Littleton, Massachusetts. The model for this third kind of group arose from the Christian Endeavor Societies and similar efforts among Unitarian and Anglican churches in England to bridge the gap between Sunday School and the adult church community. The young people's guilds also formed a national alliance.

It was easy for some churches to have both a guild and a Unity Club, with the guilds tending to be worship-oriented and the Unity Clubs study-oriented. However, most guilds were concentrated in the East, and Unity Clubs in the West. In 1890, the two national organizations, together with the Unitarian Temperance Society, joined to share a staff person at the American Unitarian Association headquarters in Boston, and to publish a newspaper entitled *Our Young People.*

These national organizations were never very strong, although the local societies comprising them flourished. At the 1895 AUA National Conference in Washington, D.C., a group of ministers discussed the possibility of creating a single national union of young people's religious societies. Despite strong youth work on the local level, they were concerned about the lack of coordinated effort. Many local societies had clubs that were independent of any national affiliation.

The ministers called a plenary meeting of all interested young people during the next Anniversary Week in May of 1896 in Boston, Massachusetts. Arnold Crompton describes the exhortations at that meeting:

> It was Thomas Van Ness who presented a plan whereby a national youth group could be formed around the ideals of worship, service, and truth. He attacked the prevailing attempts to hold young people in the churches by "pink teas," "oyster suppers," dancing parties, and dramatic shows. These were all right in their place, but should not be central. "We need to put before our young people high and strong ideals. They must be called upon to make personal exertion and to go out themselves to helpfulness and the regeneration of the world."

On May 28, 1896, the Young People's Religious Union was founded. The delegates chose "truth, worship, and service" as their cardinal principles and elected Thomas Van Ness as their first president. Eighty-six local societies were represented in the initial YPRU membership.

From the beginning, both the YPCU and the YPRU were essentially self-governing. However, it would be deceiving to assign that arrangement the weight it would have today. "Young people" in the church then were considered to be those under thirty-five. The average age of the leadership in both organizations in those early days was well over thirty, with much of the early initiative coming from young ministers. This does not mean that the tone and style of the youth organizations completely matched those of their parent bodies, though. YPCU and YPRU were created to fill a need. The young people felt that they could do some things differently by working from a self-governing institutional base within the church.

The first two decades of the Young People's Christian Union were years of growth. They probably represent the period of the Union's greatest strength. The YPCU was formally composed of state unions, and much of the organizing effort during those first few years went on at the state level. For example, during the first year, membership in the Massachusetts-Rhode Island Union leaped from seventeen to fifty-eight local unions. Membership statistics during this period are vague, however. A safe estimate might be that the YPCU had ten thousand active members at its peak during this period. The best-attended YPCU national convention took place in Boston in 1895, with six hundred delegates representing 239 unions from 27 states.

The first annual national convention of the Young People's Christian Union took place in Rochester, New York, in 1890. A major focus there, and in YPCU for many years after, was missionary activity.

YPCU's early missionary effort is one of the more dramatic

stories in the history of Universalist and Unitarian youth movements. Apparently YPCU members did not initiate it themselves, although they quickly took it to their hearts. Initiatives and prodding from ministers, who represented the Universalist convention at the YPCU gathering, seem to have started the ball rolling. Rev. Charles Ellwood Nash and Dr. Quillen Hamilton Shinn sparked the group's decision to enter the missionary field.

The Rochester YPRU convention of 1890 voted to build and support a Universalist church in Harriman, Tennessee. Historians of that convention disagree about whether the idea to do so was first proposed by Nash or by Harry Canfield, who would later become YPCU's national secretary. At any rate, it seems clear that Nash had already begun the Harriman work at the time. He had bought the land, and put some money toward the project. Nash recalled the convention in a letter:

> Thus far I had been almost solely responsible for the conduct of the enterprise, and was debating in my own mind how to proceed further. The inspiration came to me when I saw, and still more when I felt, the spirit of the young people at the Rochester Convention. Thrilled and elevated by the power of their own spiritual achievement, and ardently longing to render some more acceptable service to the church of their faith, they were more than half ready to demand to be shown some enterprise upon which they could concentrate to display and demonstrate their purpose. I had only to propose that they father the Harriman movement and the thing was done.

A thousand dollars was raised on the spot at the convention to support the work. Initial funds went to support a minister in Harriman, Rev. William H. McGlaufin. On Easter Sunday, 1892, the new church was finished and dedicated. In one year, the union had raised some $6,000 to support the construction. The idea had caught fire in the denomination and one general appeal had brought much of the money in. All totaled, the YPCU put $8,000 into the Harriman venture.

In 1894, the YPCU held its national convention at the new Tennessee site. Reports described the event as tremendously spirited, bordering on the "Pentecostal." Delegates elected Harry Canfield as national secretary, and created a "Junior Union" aimed at youth of high school age and younger. Mary Grace Webb Canfield (Harry's wife) became the first superintendent for the Junior Union. Another major event of the Harriman convention was the inauguration of a "Two Cents A Week Plan" to raise money for missionary work. The idea was to have every YPCU member contribute a dollar each year to this missionary fund. Its name was inspired by a comment by Nash: "Why, what is one dollar? It is only two cents a week for a year!"

In 1893, the YPCU hired Quillen Shinn as a national organizer. He devoted his time over the next few years to scouting out likely places for missionary activity and receiving and evaluating offers and requests for missionary work. Atlanta, Georgia, became the next site to benefit from a Universalist church built by the YPCU. The Union raised and contributed $16,000 to it, no mean sum at the turn of the twentieth century. Next, Little Rock, Arkansas, received $6,000 for a new chapel, and St. Paul, Minnesota, had a new $16,230 church constructed and called a new minister.

The home-mission activity peaked with construction of the Shinn Memorial Church in Chattanooga, Tennessee. The first minister to serve the church, Luther Robinson, had converted to Universalism after reading YPCU literature. The church was dedicated during the 1916 national convention in Chattanooga.

The YPCU also put $13,000 into the sponsorship of an itinerant Universalist preacher in Texas, "to send him abroad with a tent for his meetings," and to engage in debates about doctrinal issues. Shinn also founded, and the YPCU supported, a black Universalist church in Barton, Georgia, whose African American pastor, Rev. John W. Murphy of Barton, had converted to Universalism through the missionary literature.

Japan, then the subject of much interest in America, became the YPCU's focus for foreign missions. In 1904, the organization began contributing to the salary of a Japanese Universalist minister.

These programs of building and ministerial support were accompanied by a Mission Study Program, which distributed books on mission work and carried on general evangelizing through the mails. A large Post Office Mission was also a part of the YPCU program. For 25 years, the Union distributed some 25,000 tracts about Universalism each year to a mailing list of 1,500.

The "Two Cents A Week Plan" continued very successfully until 1917 and resulted in the creation of a permanent fund for missions. Members' interest in the missions began to wane after World War I, however. Attempts to revive the sagging fund occurred over the next thirty years under various names (Home Mission, the Legion of the Cross, and finally Church Extension), but the enthusiasm of the early part of the century never returned. However, a historical sketch published by the Union in 1939 showed that the YPCU raised an average of $2,000 a year for missions during its fifty-year history.

The YPCU's membership had a broader age range than that of the YPRU from the beginning. In the first year after its founding, the national Junior Union boasted forty chapters. They grew to become an adjunct of the Sunday School, and often included people as young as fourteen. At peak strength, the Junior Union had 112 chapters with more than 2,600 members. Junior Unions did not differ substantially from the others in style or activity, only in age. Mission work continued as a major thrust.

Harry and Mary Grace Canfield were central in this early YPCU growth. Mary Canfield worked very hard for the national YPCU in encouraging the development of the Junior Unions. In addition to their administrative and organizing efforts, the Canfields co-edited the new national YPCU publication, *Onward*. Another notable personality of these years was Lucinda White Brown, or "Auntie Brown," as YPCU members called her affectionately. She was the widow of a Universalist minister, Rev. John Stanley Brown, of Akron, Ohio, and a friend to the many YPCU members in her own area and at conventions of all kinds. When she died, she left nearly $5,000 to the YPCU—the largest single gift to the Union's endowment.

A recurrent political problem, beginning early in the YPCU, was the conflict of interest and power among various state unions and the national union, a conflict that has continued to be a source of tension in youth organizations. Many state unions were very strong and guarded their independence, particularly in the East, where the great majority of Universalist churches were concentrated. For example, although the Massachusetts State Union had favored a national body, from the beginning it considered the state union the cornerstone of membership and loyalty in YPCU. At its second meeting, in 1890, that state union passed a resolution that read,

> Resolved: that we favor a national union of young people's organizations, but feel that membership should be through state unions, and trust that the national union's constitution be so amended to allow such membership.

Finances proved a major point of controversy between the national and state groups. Delegates to national conventions would naturally get very inspired by the oratory of the speakers and the enthusiastic atmosphere. They often pledged dues or gifts to mission work far beyond the means of their groups back home. The national union would then find it necessary to dun the state unions for their commitments, which created resentment. Controversies also arose over overlapping powers and responsibilities among national and state officers and from some overt political interference with state meetings and elections on the part of national officers.

The 1898 YPCU convention in Chicago marked a turning point in resolving these disputes. The Massachusetts State Union successfully spearheaded a drive to reduce the cost and influence of the national union. The cost of putting out *Onward* was a particularly sore point, and in what became known as the "Chicago Plan," the Massachusetts delegation proposed several budget cuts, including discontinuing the positions of salaried editor and secretary for *Onward*. The measure passed, and the national union carried on with more volunteer labor than before.

Less documentation is available for the earliest years of the Young People's Religious Union than for the YPCU. In spite of claiming 4,000 members in 116 affiliated groups by 1900, the scope of the national program for Unitarian youth was very modest. At the outset, the union only employed a part-time worker to perform secretarial and administrative tasks. Only a dozen of its affiliated groups were located outside the New England and Middle Atlantic areas, so fundraising for the YPRU was conducted easily through semi-annual bazaars in Boston. The union sold life memberships for $10 each and solicited individual donations. The YPRU had 178 life members on the rolls by the 1930s, when the practice of buying such memberships had begun to die out.

The YPRU contributed a regular column to the *Christian Register*, and published a little journal called *Word and Work* in association with the AUA and the Woman's Alliance. The Union supported a certain amount of missionary work in its early days —contributing funds to struggling Unitarian churches in Dallas, Texas; Amherst, Massachusetts; and Pueblo, Colorado—though these efforts could not compare with those of the YPCU.

In 1901, the first Young People's Day was celebrated at the Isle of Shoals, marking the beginning of YPRU's long association with the conference center off the coast of Portsmouth, New Hampshire (known today as Star Island). In 1902, the YPRU formed its first district federations, modeled after the AUA district conferences in Massachusetts, New York, New Jersey, Pennsylvania, and Chicago.

Gradually the YPRU established itself on a firmer institutional base. The Union was incorporated in the Commonwealth of Massachusetts in 1911 and made a formal declaration of a trust for its funds. Conducting its first major fundraising campaign in 1914, the Union sought to establish a permanent endowment fund. The campaign raised $22,000, but the interest gained, amounting to $1,100 a year, was not sufficient to fulfill YPRU members' hopes for financial stability.

Union Programs

From its beginning, the YPRU held joint rallies with the YPCU. The first "Uni-Uni" rally occurred in 1897 at the Universalists' Columbus Avenue Church in Boston. The rallies continued, beginning the half-century of multilevel cooperation between the two groups that would eventually culminate in their merger.

Clinton Lee Scott, in his history of the Universalist Church, documents the two groups' first discussion of a joint program:

> In 1897, the annual convention of the YPCU was held in Detroit, Michigan. Rev. Jabez T. Sunderland was sent by the Unitarians as a YPCU fraternal delegate. . . . Mr. Sunderland proposed to the YPCU convention that in the future the two groups meet in joint convention. His suggestion, according to the report in *Onward*, was "greeted with cheers." There were, however, other opinions regarding this, and no action was taken. Instead a resolution was passed extending greetings to the YPRU and "invoking the blessings of Almighty God upon its endeavors after the Christian Life." Rev. Edwin C. Sweetser of Philadelphia, a staunch denominationalist and author of the pamphlet *Shall We Ally Ourselves With the Unitarians?* (in which he voiced an emphatic "*no*") was the delegate sent to the Detroit meetings from the Universalist General Convention. He was well qualified to speak for those in official positions who sought to keep clear of entangling alliances.

The quick success of these joint rallies indicates that the two groups had no great differences in activities and style on the local level. The groups were by and large affiliated with local churches, although it appears that certain aspects of "youth-adult relations" have changed little over the years. For example, one history of a YPCU state union notes,

The Board had met with a number of disappointments, especially in the number of churches which had denied them the privilege of meeting; but the Board overcame all such difficulties.

A Sunday meeting in either group would generally consist of some topic for discussion, or perhaps a speaker. Many of the notable Universalist leaders in the Boston area, such as Clarence Skinner or A.A. Miner, would take the time to address local union meetings. The evening's topic would be followed by a business session if necessary, often ending with a short worship service.

The YPCU appears to have been more devotional than the YPRU. Local Universalist unions often organized meetings around an evening of worship. Harry Adams Hersey, the historian of the YPCU's first half-century, observed,

> It could not have been organized if the religious program had been omitted. . . . The *heart* is not strangely warmed at socials, however laudable and necessary, at dances, however well conducted, or in money-raising enterprises, however proper and fruitful.

A pietistic group emerged within the early YPCU. This group, called "The Comrades of the Quiet Hour," took a particular interest in personal religious life and devotion. Yet YPCU members of that era did not renounce worldly comforts. Hersey writes, "Perhaps the most striking differences between those early conventions and the youth conferences of the post-war era today can be found in the menus. They certainly knew how to eat then." The menu for the Massachusetts State YPCU Annual Banquet of 1904 included oysters, three kinds of meat, rolls, olives, three kinds of salad, ice cream, cake, and coffee.

World War I marked the end of the initial growth period of the Unitarian and Universalist youth organizations. By the beginning of the war, both youth organizations were well established and relatively stable both in finances and membership. The war years were a time of reduced activity, as many young people went off to fight, supported and encouraged by their YPCU and YPRU friends back home. However, the regular YPRU columns in *The Christian Register* indicate that local chapters continued to function strongly.

Times were changing quickly, as evidenced by a brief note at the end of the minutes of the 1912 YPCU annual convention:

> The convention adjourned at 12:15 and the afternoon was spent at an outing at Wading River Farm, Marshfield, where lunch was served. The highpoint of the convention was the fact that the outing was made in automobiles.

When activity began to gear up again after the war, it was a new world.

The Eight O'Clock Club, while not a part of the Sunday School, grew out of it and was for several years (during the 1890s) a flourishing institution well loved by those of us in our late teens and early twenties. Its members were Toledo, Ohio, Unitarians, and our friends who attended other churches or none at all. We met on Monday evenings in the church parlor.

The programs, and they were often lively, consisted of music, recitations, dissertations on various subjects, and debates. There were usually twenty-five or more present and it didn't take refreshments to bring them out, for there were none. It just satisfied the natural desire of young people for sociability.

The Eight O'Clockers were older than me. Three or four years make a big difference at that age, so we formed another Sunday School class and had our own little social club, which met regularly in one another's homes with some outsiders who were not Unitarians. But we were not as high minded as the Eight O'Clockers for it took refreshments and prizes to hold us together.

After several years of happy and enthusiastic association, the Eight O'Clockers disintegrated, and I believe this was due to the sudden and untimely death of Harry Boss. He and Gus Fenneberg were devoted friends and leaders in the club. Harry's death cast a spirit of gloom over all, from which the club never recovered.

Another interesting, if ephemeral, outgrowth of the Sunday School was the attempt by Lydia Commander and Beth Cummings to establish a branch of the Young People's Religious Union. This must have occurred about 1903. John Haynes Holmes was at that time studying at Harvard and came to Toledo for this purpose. Bert met him at the station and brought him to our house where a group had assembled. After supper we went to the church where Mr. Holmes went competently to work and organized us into a branch of the YPRU.

At a later meeting I was assigned to speak on "What Jesus Means To Me." Although I was teaching school at the time and should have possessed some sense and ability, this seemed like an impossible task and I am sure the results were far from inspiring.

Normal Unitarian young people were not used then, if they are now, to offering prayer or exposing their innermost beliefs on religious subjects. And so the Toledo branch of the YPRU died, in spite of its now famous founder.

Lucie Harmon
Toledo, Ohio

My first real contact with Unitarian youth activities was the Young People's Religious Union of the Unitarian Church in Meadville, Pennsylvania. I arrived in Meadville in 1915, and attended the group regularly for a year or two. The membership was high school age and up. Other Meadville students attended. I was twenty-one at the time.

Total attendance at meetings must have been around twenty-five at least. Nelson Julius Springer, a Meadville student, was president of the Meadville YPRU, at least some of the time I attended it. He had briefly been an actor before attending Meadville and used to preside at meetings in full evening dress and wearing white gloves that, as I recall, could have been whiter than they were.

A meeting consisted of a service from the youth hymnal Jubilate Deo, by Charles W. Wendte, led by the president. Then we had an *outside speaker. I don't clearly recall any other activity. The church organist, Minnie Gibson, played the piano. There may have been an occasional dance, though I doubt it.*

Vincent Silliman
Meadville, Pennsylvania

It was some sixty-odd years ago in Dorchester, Massachusetts, that I became a member of the Nathaniel Hall Society of the First Parish Church. This young people's society was considered by some to be one of the outstanding groups in the country at the time.

What was it like to be a part of that group? It was to look forward eagerly from one meeting to the next. Twice a month, there was a Sunday evening devotional service with a speaker—planned and conducted by the members and often attended by a few interested adults. Once a month there was a business meeting followed by a social evening. The business was conducted with careful adherence to Robert's Rules of Order, and frequently decisions became very complex; the social evening consisted largely of dancing and good fellowship.

In those days Hi-Fi had not been developed, nor had small orchestras become important to us. We were satisfied to hire a pianist for the season and had just as much fun. Sometimes, for a special party, like the annual masquerade, we would add a drum and traps. That made for a gala occasion, with a surprising variety of costumes and much enthusiasm. The Social Committee always secured two mothers as chaperones, and the young people were careful to greet them at the beginning and say good-night to them at the end of the evening. There was nothing forced about this recognition of an accepted social custom of those days.

Once a year the "Nat Hall Society," as it was affectionately called (named for a former minister), planned and staged a dramatic performance which ran for two nights. Plays such as The Geisha Girl, The Importance of Being Ernest, The Dover Road, Charlie's Aunt, *etc., succeed in bolstering the treasury, that the Society could carry out its social service work: providing Thanksgiving baskets for needy* persons, making Christmas for a family of children who would have had none, occasionally visiting shut-ins, etc. The Treasury was also used to send delegates to the Isle of Shoals conferences. In addition to the cast, there was stage managing, lighting, advertising, publicity and programming to be done by other members—participation that strengthened the organization.

Sunday afternoon hikes, picnics (sometimes even in winter), and other impromptu gatherings were common. We belonged to and were active in the Boston Federation of the YPRU societies and attended monthly meetings in large numbers. That was before young people had their own cars. Therefore, it was necessary to use public transportation to get to meetings; sometimes an hour's trip each way with one or two transfers. It was a lark! Because we had fun being together. And because we attended these meetings and other district conferences in such large numbers, we became acquainted with other YPRU groups and were able to take part in their activities too. Many of us became active in the Federation dramatics that were staged in Boston. For many of us "Nat Hall" was the basis of our social life, as well as a wonderful experience in taking responsibility and learning how to run an organization whose membership fluctuated from about thirty-five to fifty.

YPRU Sunday was observed annually, with our members conducting the entire service—two or more in the pulpit (one preaching the sermon), one as organist, a choir of ten or twelve, and four ushers.

I suppose our average individual membership lasted only four or five years. One had to be fifteen years old to join, and then the beginning of college marked a change in interests. However, several members (commuters to college) continued active membership when they could, and the Christmas and Spring vacations brought about joyful reunions. Membership was not restricted to Unitarians but was open to interested friends.

Our activities were not limited to our own organization. There was excellent rapport with the adults of the church who were interested in what we were doing and who welcomed our participation in their activities—suppers, fairs, etc. Many of us were regular atten-

dants at church services—another opportunity to be together—and when the fiftieth anniversary of the Nathaniel Hall Society was observed in the early 1960s, there was a surprising turn-out, some members coming from a considerable distance to attend the dinner following church service.

We loved our organization and gave much of ourselves to it. In return we gained life-time friendships, and some even found their life partners.

Perhaps the most distinguishing characteristic of the Nathaniel Hall Society was its esprit de corps. *This was a heritage from previous members and was carefully nurtured by all of us.*

Katherine Hooke
Dorchester, Massachusetts

Building the Institution

FOLLOWING WORLD WAR I, a new generation assumed leadership in Unitarian and Universalist youth organizations and established a firm institutional foundation that ensured survival of the youth movement as a distinctive branch of the liberal church.

The YPRU's pre-war financial campaign had been the first step toward expanding the program beyond the Boston-area corresponding secretariat that it had been until that time. In 1917, the organization hired its first field secretary in an attempt to reach out to member groups further away from Boston.

The continental leaders of both the YPRU and the YPCU at this time were still people in their early thirties, all of them working, many married. As the war ended, Frederick May Eliot was the YPRU president, while the Universalists had just elected Helen Bisbee, the first woman president of the YPCU.

A Campaign for Cash

The Young People's Religious Union was governed at this time by a group of elected officers and a board of eighteen directors, who were elected in groups of six for three-year terms. Regional committees functioned primarily as subcommittees of this central administration, though they also sent voting representatives to YPRU board meetings. Only in its conception was this was a "continental" or even a national board. Although 15 regions, representing 228 local societies, were involved, the board was still very New England–oriented. Monthly board meetings always took place in Boston, and due to lack of travel subsidies, only New Englanders could attend. In personal correspondence, Robert Raible described his frustration at attending a YPRU board meeting in 1923, seeking to represent a region where he was among the recognized youth program leaders. He was allowed to sit in but not to participate, in spite of the absence of any other representatives. The early 1920s saw the first major shift in the age of the YPRU leadership. For the first time, all leaders were under thirty. Raible writes,

> I can recollect Charles Bolster and Ed Furber being presidents of YPRU after they were married (which means they were somewhere around thirty). I do not recollect exactly. I do remember trying to run an abortive campaign against Charles Bolster for YPRU president on the sole ground that a married man was too old to be president of YPRU.

The paid staff during the 1920s was led by one full-time executive secretary in Boston, who received a salary of $700 per year and was assisted by up to four field secretaries, located in New England, the Middle Atlantic, the Midwest, and the Pacific Coast areas. This expansion in staff was made possible by a capital drive initiated in 1920 by the American Unitarian Association, entitled The Unitarian Campaign. It was designed to be a united fundraising effort on behalf of twelve Unitarian-related organizations. Over a five-year period The Unitarian Campaign raised around $2,400,000 for the AUA and its affiliates.

The YPRU had to demonstrate to the board of prominent Unitarians managing the campaign that it had a program and a plan worth supporting. One of the main arguments in their applications hinged around the developing interest in "student work," programming for college students, within Unitarian circles. The YPRU argued for control of this area. Although the young people received less than they had requested from the Unitarian Campaign, the money donated made a substantial difference.

An initial donation of $5,000 in 1921 was used to eliminate a deficit and hire an office secretary and new field workers. The Endowment Fund Drive of 1914 had marked an effort to establish a permanent, guaranteed annual budget for YPRU, since contributions from affiliated groups would support only a small percentage of the programs YPRU wanted. Donations from the Unitarian Campaign increased the endowment to $50,000 by 1925. The interest from this sum was still not enough to free the YPRU from the necessity of annual fundraising, however.

Young People's Week

Since their beginning, Youth Sundays have ranked among the most enduring youth programs within Unitarianism or Universalism. The YPCU presented the first "Young People's Day" on January 31, 1892. Although the idea was propagated far and wide among YPCU groups, the Unitarians were quite slow picking it up. Once they did, it quickly became an annual institution. A 1931 YPRU handbook describes the origins of Young People's Week:

> It was in 1917 that the idea of Young People's Sunday was first conceived by Rev. Houghton Page, one of the many Unitarian ministers who at that time began to show a real interest in the activities of our YPRU. He requested that the first Sunday in December be observed as Young People's Day in all Unitarian churches, and that the young people be allowed to take a prominent part in the church services. The response at that time was small, and it was not until 1921 that the officers of the YPRU, realizing the infinite possibilities of Mr. Page's suggestion, began to campaign, first with and then through the individual members of the organization for the observance of Young People's Day as an annual event for churches.
>
> In 1921, about a hundred churches observed it in some way, and in about forty churches the local members of the

YPRU took part in or took charge of the service. Each year the response has been greater, and as the young people have proved beyond a doubt their growing interest, power, and capability in the work of our churches, the feeling of skepticism on the part of the ministers and the church members has diminished until now Young People's Sunday is observed annually by at least two-thirds of our churches, and is looked forward to, not as something to be endured for the sake of the young folks, but as something to be enjoyed with them.

Young People's Sunday in Boston became the inaugural event of the annual Young People's Week, which included parties, fundraising events, a dance, and a play with a YPRU cast that was presented downtown and in several suburbs. Young People's Week developed into a major fundraiser for the Union.

YPCU Programs and Prospects

Since the watershed 1898 convention in Chicago, the YPCU's financial troubles and political controversies between the national and the state unions had gradually receded. By 1910, the organization's financial health had improved to the point that a full-time secretary for field work was appointed. Robert Etz, who made a success of the job, would go on to become superintendent of the Universalist General Convention. Carl Elsner succeeded him as field secretary, followed by Stanley Manning, who was appointed to the new position of director of young people's work within the Universalist General Convention in 1919.

The structure of the YPCU at this time was similar to the structure that Liberal Religious Youth would later adopt. A national board governed YPCU affairs, with one full-time staff member, centered in Boston but mandated to travel. During and immediately following World War I, YPCU experienced a drop in membership and local group activity. An eventual consequence was consolidation of some smaller state unions, like the Rhode Island

Union, which joined the stronger Massachusetts Union in 1926.

Though the "Two Cents A Week Plan" for missions, begun in 1894, had remained a successful YCPU fundraising program for two decades, income had declined during the war years. The name "Two Cents A Week" was changed in 1917 to "Home Mission," in the hope that a new image might revive donations. Later that year, when "Home Mission" proved a little too lackluster, the program was renamed "Legion of the Cross."

In 1922, Clifford and Margaret Stetson, Universalist missionaries and members of YPCU, began a nine-year assignment in Japan, supported by mission funds. The Junior Unions later supported the education of some Japanese girls through the Stetsons.

Yet the postwar years forced the YPCU to manage its finances more stringently. The Union's hopes rested on the Universalist General Convention's ambitious 1919 campaign for funds, unabashedly entitled "The Million Dollar Drive." Following that drive's successful completion, the convention began to support 50 percent of the YPCU budget directly. Additional support was promised as insurance against future financial difficulties. *Onward*, the YPCU publication, routinely encountered financial distress, and alternated between a sixteen-page weekly and a sporadic newsletter as a result. Aid from the Universalist Publishing House occasionally helped keep it going.

The postwar decline in YPCU membership leveled off at between four and five thousand, although exact figures are hard to determine. The Universalist and Unitarian groups each experienced a slow drop in the average age of their members during the 1920s. Hersey noted that the average age of a YPCU board member in 1895 was twenty-nine and a half. In those early days of the Union, when it was supporting four or five mission churches, paying their ministers' salaries, and carrying on the Post Office Mission, the YPCU leadership consisted of ministers or prominent lay people in their late twenties or early thirties. As these responsibilities gradually fell away, it became apparent that the members of the organization (who were generally younger than the leadership) might respond more favorably to leaders of their own age. The YPCU convention at Ferry Beach in Saco, Maine, in 1919 saw the first influx of people in their teens. What Hersey calls "the epoch of youth only" was beginning.

Summer Conferences and Conventions

Conferences have always been an important dimension of Unitarian and Universalist youth programs. Without the motivation of conference experiences, many local youth groups, and certainly the regional and continental organizations, would have withered away.

The first weekend conference sponsored by the YPRU at the Isles of Shoals (Star Island) was held in 1921. Since that longer conference received favorable feedback, and since the Union was back on its feet financially as a result of the Unitarian Campaign, planners decided to try a week-long conference in 1922. The response was overwhelming. Two hundred and fifty delegates attended, including many from outside New England. The experience of that week had a far-reaching effect in the Unitarian churches. In 1923, the Young People's Conference was expanded to two full weeks and held in conjunction with the YPRU annual meeting. So began a tradition of YPRU national conferences at Star Island that would continue until 1940.

The YPCU had long sponsored extended summer camps and conventions for young people at such places as Ferry Beach, in Saco, Maine, and Murray Grove in New Jersey. The Universalists' national convention moved around from year to year between sites as far-flung as Chicago, Minneapolis, Detroit, and even Los Angeles. This contrasted with the Unitarian pattern, which made Young People's Week at The Shoals the annual Mecca.

The Shoals experience led to the initiation of other summer conferences. Districts sponsored mid-year and spring weekend events, and by 1924 there were five other week-long summer conferences: one at Rowe Camp in Western Massachusetts, two in the

Midwest, and two in California, with the latter leading to the formation of a California District YPRU.

The relationship of the Young People's Religious Union to Rowe Camp was an important one, for the founding and growth of Rowe was intimately tied to a desire for Unitarian summer camps for young people in Western Massachusetts and Connecticut. After Rowe hosted some official YPRU summer conferences the Rowe board invited the president of the YPRU to sit in as an ex-officio member.

The national YPRU's first unrestricted bequest came from the estate of a resident of Deerfield, Massachusetts, who had maintained a long interest in and affection for the young people's programs at Rowe. Lucy E. Henry, who died on Young People's Sunday in 1927, left small bequests to institutions in the town of Rowe itself. However, a substantial portion of her estate, amounting to one-half of the residue after other bequests and expenses, was left to the Young People's Religious Union. It amounted to $1,235.79.

The year after "Miss Henry's" death, Unitarian Rowe Camp, Inc., decided to purchase the Bonnie Blink Cottage and the land upon which it stood to establish the camp as a permanent institution. The original deed to the camp land specified that in the event that Rowe Camp dissolved, the title should revert to the Young People's Religious Union. In view of the fact that Henry's bequest came as a result of the "Rowe Spirit," and considering the decision to purchase the camp land, the YPRU board elected to donate one half of the bequest back to Rowe Camp for the possible construction of a dining hall.

By 1934, the Rowe summer conference had become so successful that many feared it would rival the national convention at The Shoals. The two events were carefully scheduled at different times.

These early conferences and conventions encountered the same occasional problems with rules that contemporary conferences do. Dana Greeley recalled one flap at Star Island involving conferees hauling their mattresses out onto the roof of the Oceanic Hotel in order to sleep outside. The conventions and the summer camps provided unusual opportunities for young people to travel, as they do today. A convention was an occasion requiring months of saving and fundraising, culminating in an exciting train trip, since state delegations often rode together. The long, expensive trips to conventions stirred up controversy, then as now. Hersey replies sharply to such criticism in his fiftieth-anniversary memoir of the Young People's Christian Union:

> Hundreds of thousands of dollars for traveling expenses and joy riding! Why this waste? Might they not better have stayed home, and given the money to the church or to missions? The answer is that, first, the money would not have been given, and second, it is that our young people knew a good investment when they saw one. No money ever spent by our young people produced richer returns. Before travel was possible for most of our youth, in the ordinary course of life, the conventions made it possible; opened up new worlds, broadened the mind, quickened the sympathies, enlarged the interests, benefited the whole man, and blessed ultimately the whole denomination.

The Student Federation of Religious Liberals

In response to growing concern about youth program "student work," a Joint Student Committee was created in 1923 to establish young people's societies in every church, in conjunction with a joint AUA-YPRU campaign. That committee, composed of representatives from the AUA, the Alliance of Women, the Unitarian Ministerial Union, the Layman's League, and the YPRU, was charged with avoiding duplication of efforts while collectively promoting student work.

A substantial number of college students took part in the YPCU and the YPRU, and various "Channing Clubs" and other YPRU branches were active on campuses. However, no effort was made to create an organization that would specifically address the needs of college students until 1923, when the Student Federation of Religious Liberals (SFRL) was created.

The instigator of this new venture was a minister—Rev. Harold B. Speight, an Englishman and the minister of King's Chapel in Boston: Speight was instrumental in declaring the second week of the 1923 Shoals Young People's Convention a "Student Week." A program directed at college students alone became Speight's pet project, and he managed to sell the idea to the 265 liberal religious students (representing 75 schools from 20 states and Canada) assembled on the island. Robert Raible became the first president of the fledgling organization, heading up an eleven-person Executive Committee. Alfred Hobart was appointed as a full-time, salaried executive secretary. Speight attended the Unitarian General Conference that year looking for funding and came back with a promise of financial support for SFRL.

Both YPRU and YPCU decided to lend financial and moral support as well. SFRL became a federation of the YPRU, with two representatives on its board. The organization began with eight affiliated member groups and thirty-one individual members.

Hobart traveled extensively to colleges during that first year of adequate funding, then left the position when he was accepted as a student at the Meadville Theological School. Raible took over the executive secretary job, but the organization could only afford him half-time. Granville Hicks, a prominent YPCU leader and editor of *Onward*, served as president during that second year. SFRL produced *The Student Leader*, a monthly four-page glossy newsletter, and distributed *Onward*. The executive secretary also corresponded with and distributed material on the Leyden International Bureau, an international corresponding secretariat of liberal religious young people based in Holland. This represented the North Americans' first contact with attempts in Europe to bring liberal religious youth together across national boundaries.

Speight was never again as successful in raising money from denominational sources for the venture as he was during that first year. The second annual SFRL conference, held at Mount Holyoke College, drew 150 students from forty schools, including Congregationalists, Quakers, and Episcopalians. Toward the end of the second year, SFRL suffered a crushing blow: YPRU, disenchanted with SFRL's program and suspicious about the number of non-Unitarians in its membership, severed its funding. When Russell Wood became the third president of SFRL, there was not enough money left to hire a secretary, so he did all the office work himself.

In 1926, the Student Federation of Religious Liberals was disbanded. It had managed to hold three annual conferences: in 1923 at Star Island in New Hampshire, in 1924 at Mount Holyoke in Massachusetts, and in 1925 at Phillips Andover Academy in Massachusetts. It was a valiant try, one that would not be attempted again on any national scale for twenty years.

A Financial Crunch

As the 1920s came to an end, both youth groups began to feel pressured for funds again. The Unitarian Campaign money had expired in 1925. A new drive began that year under the name "Unitarian Foundation" and young people responded enthusiastically. When that year's Star Island convention learned of the campaign, some two hundred young people pledged $1,237.00 within three hours.

The Unitarian Foundation pledged a $10,000 grant to the YPRU in the 1927 fiscal year, but expectations that it would ever be paid were low. The foundation budgeted $4,000, but in the end contributed only $2,504.50.

A special appeal to pay off the 1927 debts was needed, as were budget cuts. Two field-secretary positions merged into one, and YPRU sounded out the Laymen's League on the possibility of sharing the expenses and time of the more far-flung field workers. The YPRU magazine, *Pegasus*, which had been under-subscribed since its inception in 1926, also had to cut back.

As 1929 began, Foundation monies were exhausted. The YPRU and the Laymen's League decided to embark upon a joint fundraising effort to model co-operative fundraising and help establish a permanent endowment that could meet YPRU's annual budget needs in perpetuity.

This campaign, entitled the "Maintenance Fund," adopted a goal of $406,000, with YPRU endowment support a priority. But soon afterward, in October, 1929, the stock market crashed. Although the YPRU and YPCU had not invested sufficient resources in the markets to be badly hurt, Unitarian and Universalist institutions suffered losses. The crash and the Great Depression that followed brought an end to the Maintenance Fund and to any further capital fundraising efforts toward an independently endowed youth organization.

⁓

From 1921 until about 1929 I was a member (and a one-time president) of the Lyon Guild, which was the official name of the young people's group in the First Parish in Brookline, Massachusetts. The meetings were usually business affairs: arranging programs, assisting the church where possible, etc. Each year the group put on a dramatic production in the hall adjacent to and part of the church. Also, each spring, the group went on a Sunday afternoon and evening picnic at the country or seashore homes of parents.

During the winter, we had Sunday evening meetings preceded by suppers that were prepared by members. I remember I became noted for strawberry shortcake, made from scratch in the church kitchen on Sunday afternoon. I fear that the group's activities were chiefly on the social side rather than the religious or ecclesiastical.

Before that, I was a member of the "Fraternity" at All Souls Church in Roxbury, the activities of which were similar to those described above.

In 1926, 1927, and 1928 I was president of the national YPRU, the duties of which took all my available time, so I did not partici-

pate in local society activities after that, other than visiting different local societies, chiefly in New England but on a few occasions in the Midwest and New York areas. I preached the sermon on three successive youth Sundays in Brookline, Massachusetts; Jamestown, New York; and Billerica, Massachusetts, and was active in connection with the YPRU summer conferences, chiefly at Star Island.

I then believed, and still believe, that if young people (and by that I mean in ages from seventeen or eighteen to twenty-three or twenty-four) can organize a group closely affiliated with a church, and if that group can assemble at monthly gatherings, such activities strengthen the life of the members and also the corporate life of the church. I know that my experiences in the Lyon Guild, and later in the National YPRU work, meant a great deal to me and enriched my life as much as anything I did then.

Charles S. Bolster
Brookline, Massachusetts

Ann Rheiner: I was a member of the YPCU at the First Universalist Church of Wakefield, Massachusetts, from 1922 to 1927. It was a very small group of young people. Mostly the minister helped to form YPCUs, and in our case he was our consultant.

We formed an organization, held elections for officers, and chose committees for worship services, a YPCU representative in the New England organization, a Social Committee, and a fundraising chairman. We raised our own budget, including $500 each year for the last two years during which I was a member, which we contributed to the church.

We met on Sunday nights. The programs were part devotional and part educational. Every person in the group took a turn being the speaker, and then we brought in outsiders.

Conard Rheiner: We were married at the Wakefield Church. I was a student at Tufts, and one of my fellow students was the president of the Wakefield YPCU. He knew that I'd had plenty of experience as an actor, and that I was a professional magician and *entertainer, and so he hired me for fifty dollars to be in their play. That was a considerable amount of money at the time, although it represented eight trips to Wakefield. That's where we met.*

Ann: In about 1920 we pledged to raise $500 toward the budget of the church. We did it by giving these plays—three a year, running for three nights each. We also got permission to have social dancing in the downstairs vestry because this town of 15,000 had a dance hall with a bad name.

We participated in the New England organization of YPCU and cooperated with the national office in Boston.

We had anywhere from fifty to seventy-five people at these conventions. I'll never forget the first one I went to at Concord, New Hampshire. My present sister-in-law and I (we were chums then) were placed in a home of one of the prominent people in the church. We had the most beautiful bedroom and breakfast brought to us in bed the next morning with a rose on the tray.

Conard: You have to put that period in perspective because there was nothing to compete. We did have movies, and we did have dance halls, but middle class families frowned upon their children going to dance halls. No radio, no television.

Ann: I remember the church Board of Trustees up in arms about the foxtrot and the tango.

Something else we did in Wakefield was that we initiated an organization made up of young people's groups from the Congregationalist, Methodist, Baptist, and Episcopal churches that met once a month for an ecumenical worship service, a "sing-together," and once to put on a play, The Admirable Creighton, *by James M. Barrie, in the high school auditorium.*

I was just thinking, as we worked on the plans for our fiftieth wedding anniversary, how many of those people we have kept in touch with over all these years. YPCU meant a great deal to us.

Conard: And three out of the young people's group that I was in are in the UU ministry today. And two out of Ann's group.

Conard and Ann Rheiner
Wakefield, Massachusetts

Cooperation at Home and Abroad

At the 1929 Young People's Christian Union convention in Atlanta, Georgia, Dorothy Tilden Spoerl was elected president of a Union that was being forced to make serious cutbacks, particularly in its budget for *Onward*. Unlike the Unitarians, the YPCU's organizational strength was not concentrated in a few urban areas. The Universalist organization was more spread out and did not have the urban fundraising activities or support from a mother church that the Unitarian youth organization enjoyed. Money had to come from the state and local unions, but it was not coming.

The buildup to the 1929 convention was notable for the fact that one faction of the YPCU was strongly pushing for an organic union with the YPRU as a solution to the Union's financial problems.

Overtures to Merger

Speculation about a possible YPRU-YPCU merger was quite common during the late 1920s, even before economic pressures became a factor. In 1927, the two organizations began to exchange delegates to their respective conventions. This had been a common practice when the organizations were run by young ministers, but the exchanges had become more sporadic during World War I.

From 1927 to 1928, the two Unions also held conferences of their national officers to compare notes on subjects of mutual in-

terest and discuss future cooperation. The Universalists first suggested organic union of the two groups in proposals published in
Onward in 1928 and 1929. The idea met with Universalist opposition, and the Unitarians displayed no great enthusiasm for it, but
the conversation continued. In 1930, a joint committee of six
members invited forty Unitarian and Universalist young people to
a series of meetings to discuss a possible merger. The meetings
proved inconclusive, however, and the idea was laid to rest for a
few more years.

During the early 1930s, Dana Greeley and Max Kapp were the
presidents of the YPRU and the YPCU, respectively. Both would
later be involved in the final Unitarian/Universalist merger and
would work together within the UUA administration. Greeley recalled that his first serious reflections on the real possibilities of
Unitarian/Universalist merger happened in the context of the
youth movement. He recalled meeting with Kapp and others in the
home of John van Schaick, editor of the Universalist journal *The
Christian Leader* and talking long into the night about the implications of a merger.

The American Unitarian Association and the Universalist
General Convention were engaged in cooperative ventures. They
had appointed commissions on interdenominational relations and
were entertaining the idea of establishing a "Free Church of America."
That was not to be an AUA-UGC merger as such but a wider union
of religious liberals of various faiths.

With Greeley as president, the YPRU set up its own Committee
on Interdenominational Relations, which made a variety of recommendations for closer co-operation between the YPRU and the
YPCU. The committee favored parallel commissions within these
two youth organizations to "formulate a plan or plans for progressive co-operation and to apply to young people's work to the extent
practicable the plan of the Free Church of America."

In 1933, the establishment of a Joint Commission on Social
Responsibility became an important step in that direction. Other
recommendations from the Committee on Interdenominational

Relations involved membership overlap and co-operation where only one of the groups was active in a given area. The committee suggested forming only one group in areas where none had existed before. It also advocated joint attendance at all summer conferences and considered the possibility of merging the YPCU's *Onward* with the YPRU's News.

Clinton Lee Scott described a further flurry of merger activity later in the 1930s:

> The next definite action came from the Unitarian group. William E. Gardner, in an article in the *Christian Leader* of August 17, 1935, reported that "the YPRU, at its annual meeting in May, 1935, voted to effect an organic union with the YPCU if the YPCU so desired." Reports from the YPCU convention held at Ferry Beach, Maine that July gave evidence that the Universalist youth also desired merger, but under pressure from denominational officials action was "postponed" until another year.

The vision of a Free Church of America was never realized. In responding to that vision, however, youth movement leaders had experiences that significantly influenced the future course of the Unitarian and Universalist movements. The enthusiasm and the increased co-operation that characterized the two youth movements during this period would be renewed and re-created twenty-five years later in the merger process that would create the Unitarian Universalist Association.

The Peace Caravans

Members of both the YPRU and the YPCU took part in an impressive social-responsibility project during the 1930s. With help from the American Friends Service Committee as well as Robert Dexter, executive secretary of the AUA's Department of Social Relations, the two youth organizations sponsored a Peace Caravan over the five summers between 1931 and 1935.

"Peace" was a cause that encompassed many of the international issues in the news during the early 1930s. The international arms buildup, the ineffectiveness of the League of Nations, the unwillingness of the United States to enter the World Court, and the rise of Hitler all pointed to the possibility of another major war. In 1926, the American Friends Service Committee began a program in which students would travel in pairs for between seven and nine weeks around a relatively small geographic area of the United States. Using second-hand cars and generally camping out, they would seek to arrange speaking engagements for themselves on the subject of peace with anyone who would listen to them.

The YPRU had to raise around $700 annually to sponsor a Peace Caravan. Following an unsuccessful attempt in 1930, the 1931 fundraising and recruitment effort succeeded in putting the first Peace Caravan on the road. Some of the flavor and spirit of the caravan experience is captured in a selection from the diary kept by John Brigham and Homer Thomas as they traveled around Ohio in 1934:

> Friday—July 28—Brite and Fair—Warm—We packed camp today, made our final visit with our host and hostess, gorged ourselves at an enormous dinner, and moved to Covington in the afternoon. Covington is a progressive little town of 1800 inhabitants.
>
> Tonight we are in a city park, with wading pools, horse troughs, and everything. We took a bath about 11 pm in the horse trough in order to be sweet and clean when calling on the local highlights in the morning.
>
> Before going to sleep Homer and I had a long discussion on the merits and demerits of caravanning . . . .
>
> Friday, July 29—This morning we tramped the streets of Covington looking for an honest man. Finally we found him, a Legion man who opposed all Communists. We talked, told him our object, convinced him we were not Communists; so we have decked that rumor.
>
> Also we arranged meetings at the Congregational Christian Church, the Presbyterian Church, and the Kiwanis Club.

There may be others but we haven't found them. The Evangelistic Mission Church is engaged so we can't lead them in fervent prayer.

In the evening, we were discovered by a family of transients from California. (We are camped in a community pk. and tourist camp.) The couple wanted to play bridge and were feeling sad. They had been away from Cal. three months and were dying for a game. So we agreed and played a long rubber. It was nice for a change and made us take our minds off peace for a bit.

Local Groups and Conference Experience

The style, content, and degree of formality of local UU youth group programming have changed over the years. The relationships, loyalties, and learning experienced by individual local group members in YPRU and YPCU do not seem very different from the experiences of any other generation, however. In the earliest years, local YPCU programs tended to be more devotional than those of the YPRU. However, by the 1920s, "program prompters" published by the YPCU national headquarters reflected a move toward more varied and secular topics. One program booklet lists suggestions under such categories as "Work," "Play," "Thought," and "Worship."

Nevertheless, published YPCU material remained predominately worship-oriented until the 1940s. The head office would also include material on YPCU mission work, biblical themes, and the occasional social topic. Devotional meetings in both the Unitarian and Universalist groups included spirited hymn-singing. Each of the unions had its own "national hymn." The one sung by the Young People's Christian Union was entitled "Follow the Gleam":

To the knights in the days of old
Keeping watch on the mountain height
Came a vision of Holy Grail
And a voice throughout the waiting night –
Follow, follow, follow the gleam

Banners unfurled o'er all the world.
Follow, follow, follow the gleam
Of the chalice that is the Grail.
And we who would serve the King,
And loyally Him obey
In the consecrate silence know
That the challenge still holds today.
Follow, follow, follow the gleam,
Standards of worth o'er all the earth,
Follow, follow, follow the gleam
Of the light that shall bring the dawn.

The Young People's Religious Union hymn was sung to the tune of "Land of Hope and Glory":

Forward shoulder to shoulder
Fling the banner of Youth
On through worship and service
To the glorious truth.
Light of our torch wide-shining
Colors always unfurled,
Strength, vision, and courage
We pledge to the life of the world.
Strength, vision, and courage . . . .
We pledge to the life of the world.
Far horizons are calling.
Here humanity cries,
Deep in the unfathomed darkness
High in the radiant skies.
Onward, questing and daring,
Mighty our chorus is hurled.
Strength, vision, and courage
We pledge to the life of the world.
Strength, vision, and courage
We pledge to the life of the world.

A local group meeting that was primarily devotional might include some innovation designed to make the service less serious than the service for adults. One group's records indicate the youth used a "Train Service," with the order of service designed like a train stopping at various stations.

A topic-oriented local meeting might have a single speaker or a variety of group members contributing to discussion around a topic. Two examples of YPCU local group programs from the 1920s are offered below:

May 25
Leader: Miss Mildred Darrah
Topic: The Coming Summer
"What I Want To Do And Why"—Mr. Jas. Walters
"What I Should Do If I Could"—Mr. Allen Carpenter
"Lessons Of The Ball Park"—Mr. George Kennedy
"A Trip With The Socialists"—Mr. Watson Davis Solo

June 8
Leader: Miss Ruth Asley
Topic: My Summer in a Garden
"My Maryland Farm"—The President of the Union
"Weeds"—Dr. Small
"The Inspiration of Yellow Clay"—Mr. Van Schank
Symposium: City Gardens—The Members Solo

Conference events have a more familiar ring; youth-conference chaos seems to be a constant over time. Minutes from the YPCU annual conference of October, 1934, in Worcester, Massachusetts, convey some of the spirit of these gatherings:

A cafeteria supper was served at 6:30 which was followed by an informal social and dance. Bob Sproul chased around Worcester and drummed up an orchestra when the scheduled musicians failed to appear. During the evening, Vol. 1, No. 1 of *Oooh! Scandal!* appeared. To all intents and purposes, the paper was to be a summary of the convention doings from day to day, but the editorship was placed in the hands of a person with a distorted sense of humor, and he changed the intent of the paper, making it much lighter than was intended . . . . On Saturday morning, due to a two-inch fall of snow, the proposed picnic was cancelled and an in-door program was substituted. Before the group broke up at the church, Robert Barber led the 11:30 candlelight service in the church, where he detailed some of his experiences in the Rhode Island Insane Asylum.

Nationally, as the administration of AUA President Louis Cornish (1927 to 1937) neared its close, the YPRU enjoyed cordial relationships with the administration. The past president of the YPRU received an automatic seat on the AUA board, and an AUA representative usually sat in on the YPRU executive meetings. The young people remained torn between needing denominational support and contact and desiring to remain free from denominational control. However, the YPRU leaders from that period recall the denomination and the youth group basically trusting each other's programs, support, and good intentions.

Of course, the age of the participants was still as much as ten years older than the age of today's youth leaders, although the general trend was toward younger members. Dana Greeley was twenty-two when he was elected president of YPRU in 1931, and Max Kapp was twenty-seven at his election that same year.

The patterns of the previous twenty years remained relatively unchanged. The YPRU, for example, still had 65 percent of its membership concentrated in New England and along the Atlantic Coast.

Both the YPRU and the YPCU remained strong within the limits of their finances and their geographic boundaries. There was some fraying at the edges of this pattern, however. In 1935, following an appraisal of field work needs, the YPRU eliminated the positions of field secretaries. The work they had done was to be taken over by board of directors members on subsidized field trips. That approach did not succeed in encouraging and serving local groups.

The stage was set for a change.

The International Youth Movement

Although the international liberal religious youth movement began in the early 1920s, significant North American youth involvement with Europe didn't emerge until the 1930s, when it was bolstered by the personal international involvement of AUA president Louis Cornish and his administration.

The first attempt to form an international liberal religious youth organization resulted in the Leyden International Bureau, founded in 1923. Following World War I, Europe, particularly Germany, experienced a "youth culture" phenomenon similar to what would appear in North America in the 1960s. Benjamin Zablocki quotes from a paper by a member of the *Bruderhof*, the most durable communal group to emerge from the German Youth Movement, describing the atmosphere of the time:

> Germany in those inflation-ridden post-war years, amid the fragments of Wilhelminian pomp and ambition, was a vast California of cults, crusades, causes, and movements. The younger generation, almost in a body, rejected the bourgeois ways of its elders, and hiked out into the country with rucksacks and short pants, a little like co-educational senior scouts, but with a messianic mission. This was the German Youth Movement.

Along with the "back to nature" groups, Germany had national student organizations such as the Student Christian Movement and the *Studentenschft*, which called itself "a national self-governing and self-supporting student democracy."

The first representative gathering of the International Congress of Free Christians and Other Religious Liberals since the end of World War I was held in Leyden, The Netherlands, in 1922. Dr. K. H. Roessingh of the Netherlands was appointed president of the Congress at that time. He took the initiative in organizing a youth branch, naming it the Leyden International Bureau (LIB).

For the first ten years of its existence, the LIB, centered in Utrecht, Netherlands, operated primarily through "pen-pal" correspondence. Young people within the free religious movement in Germany organized themselves into the National League of German Free Thinking Youth in 1924. In 1927, when the next International Congress was held in Prague, Czechoslovakia, the two youth groups made contact.

Two small LIB conferences were held in 1928 and 1929, and the Bureau met again in conjunction with the International Congress of 1932 in St. Gal, Switzerland. The German group participated in the 1929 conference and there officially joined the LIB. As political tensions between Germany and France increased in the early 1930s, the free religious youth in Germany became more involved in peace study and action. They arranged international meetings with French youth, called "tours of peace." They studied the writings and the deeds of Gandhi, whom a group of free religious youth succeeded in meeting during his stay in Europe in the fall of 1931.

In 1933, the Nazi government dissolved all youth organizations in Germany except for the Hitler Youth. Members of the *Bund der Freireligioesen Jugend Deutschlands* buried the flag of their group on the grounds of their "youth home" in Mainz. It would be twelve years before the flag could be dug up again and given to the leaders of the post-war free religious youth.

Like the North American youth organizations, the Leyden International Bureau member groups were composed of young adults in their twenties and early thirties. Until 1934, the bureau's tasks of correspondence, conference organizing, and modest publishing were done informally out of Utrecht. The newly christened International Association for Liberal Christianity and Religious Freedom held its 1934 congress in Copenhagen, a meeting that marked the beginning of a period of renewal for the youth organization.

An international youth camp was planned to coincide with the 1934 Copenhagen congress, and for the first time, YPRU and the YPCU sent delegates. The 1934 meeting elected an Executive Committee and created a secretariat for the Leyden International

Bureau. Annual conferences were planned. The Swiss sponsored the first one in 1935 on the theme "Youth and the World of Today."

The North Americans returned that year to Switzerland, inviting the European youth the following year to Star Island for the 1936 Leyden Bureau conference in conjunction with the YPRU convention. Two hundred and twenty young people from six countries attended, including fifty-four from Europe. The highly successful conference represented a peak of international interest among young religious liberals.

The plans for renewal that had begun during the 1934 Copenhagen conference—held in the face of Hitler's rise to power in Germany—culminated finally in 1938 at Leersum, Holland, when the Leyden International Bureau was re-organized into the International Religious Fellowship (IRF). Jeff Campbell of the YPCU, one of twenty-eight American delegates attending that conference, was elected the first president. Campbell was once of the AUA's pioneer African American ministers. Donald Harrington of the YPRU became the editor of the new organization's publication, *Forward Together*. However, with World War II breaking out the following year, IRF quickly became little more than a dream. The IRF conference of 1939, at Arcegno, Switzerland, ended only three weeks prior to the hostilities. Its theme was "The Demand of God to a Confused Generation." It would be seven years before the IRF could hold any more ongoing conferences and work camps.

I was a member of the YPCU youth group in Galesburg, Illinois, all during my high school and college days in the 1920s. I think perhaps ours was an unusual group since Galesburg was the home of Lombard College (whose charter is now the Lombard part of Meadville Lombard), so our YPCU was made up of both high school and college students.

We met at the campus and walked down to the church, where we were joined by the members coming from other directions. For the most part we took the meetings seriously, even without adult super-vision. We tended to follow the program suggestions of the national organization, but when they turned out to be dull we would in-evitably turn to our two favorite questions for debate. The arguments remained hot and heavy no matter how often we discussed them. Heredity versus environment was one of the questions; the other was whether the intellect or the emotions have the greater control over human behavior.

I think the reason for our long-lasting success with a viable group was the fact that we took part in the district (in those days, state) meetings, where we tried our political wings. And a few of us man-aged to get to various of the national meetings. The Illinois YPCU of those days contributed a considerable number of people to the na-tional board, to national offices, and to the ministry.

Perhaps another reason for our success was that high schools in those days, at least in Illinois, did not offer a forum for the discussion of wide-ranging questions, and therefore anything of social or politi-cal interest would end up in the youth group meetings.

What did we gain from it? A certain degree of facility in speak-ing to sundry topics, prepared or unprepared, but not too often a push in the direction of gaining further knowledge before continuing. A sense of loyalty to Universalism, in part from occasional service to the church, but more often from our excitement over the programs of the state group. If we had a devotion in those days, it was to the cause of peace, but it was more words than action, largely for lack of con-certed action on the state or national level.

For most of us the high point of the year was Youth Sunday, when we planned the entire service (once more without adult leadership, since none seemed to be forthcoming), and elected one of our num-ber to preach the entire sermon. It was a coveted position.

Unfortunately we did not branch out to acquaintance with the Unitarians (which would have our souls good due to the more liberal stance of the Western Conference of Unitarians), though summer conferences at the state level, to which we were addicted, introduced us to such Unitarian greats as Robert Dexter and Curtis Reese.

I still hold, and I'm sure the others do as well, warm memories of our gatherings at the church, despite the fact that we rarely had a group of over fifteen or twenty. In recent years I have chanced across some of these people as they have turned up at various meetings where I have been on a program (some of them no longer Unitarian Universalist, some of them still active in our Association). Always the "do you remember?" questions include not only our high school and college days but our explorations of the world of religion and social justice work done together in the YPCU.

Dorothy Tilden Spoerl
Galesburg, Illinois

Organization and Readjustment

THE JOINT SLOGAN of the American Unitarian Association and the Young People's Religious Union during the 1920s and 1930s reflected a close relationship between the larger denomination and its youth movement. It proclaimed, "The spirit of youth in the life of the church is the hope of the world!" Frederick May Eliot was asked to use this slogan for the title of the anniversary sermon at the AUA May Meetings (what we now call General Assembly) of 1935. It showed a brave optimism This ceremonial optimism was a brave show in view of a rather depressing institutional outlook for the Unitarian and Universalist churches and their youth affiliates—a declining membership, financial weakness, and insufficient leadership.

American Unitarian Youth

The Unitarians resolved to undertake a major shift to reverse the tide. James Luther Adams, minister of the Unitarian Church in Wellesley Hills, Massachusetts, and Kenneth McDougall, a prominent lay member of the same church, were convinced of the need for a Commission of Appraisal to completely re-evaluate the structure and goals of the AUA. They dashed up and down the East Coast in the spring of 1934 to drum up support for the idea, which became a reality during that year's May Meetings.

Rev. Frederick May Eliot of St. Paul, Minnesota, chaired the commission, which undertook a thorough and far-reaching evaluation of the denomination. In 1936, the Commission of Appraisal published a report and recommendations that were to drastically alter the shape of the Unitarian movement. Like everything else, the approach to youth programming came under close scrutiny.

From the AUA's point of view, a number of problems stood out. The denomination had no direct control over the YPRU, an independent AUA affiliate that raised much of its own money, Yet it was the major AUA-affiliated program dealing with young people. The YPRU had always employed a full-time office manager and field representatives. Neither the AUA nor the YPRU had the resources to increase the staff. Yet, the existing organization seemed unable to meet the needs of the variety of age groups included within the rubric of "youth," particularly those of college age.

The Commission of Appraisal's recommendations waffled on the question of whether the AUA would try to take more direct responsibility for youth programming. However, the commission was clear about wanting to see the program grow to become truly national in scale. On the one hand, it opposed the AUA taking on the task of student functions and programming in any given area. Those were to be treated as local and regional responsibilities. On the other hand, the commission suggested that the AUA work closely with its Department of Education in whatever responsibility it assumed over student programming.

The Commission of Appraisal approved of AUA participation in some inter-agency directional efforts and recommended giving young people more direct recognition and responsibility within the denomination. As an affiliate organization, the YPRU received voting status at the annual AUA meeting and was entitled to send permanent appointees to the AUA Nominating Committee.

In 1936, the AUA appointed a five-member committee to reorganize student work in accordance with the Commission of Appraisal's suggestions. That committee's work led to the formation, in 1938, of an inter-agency group called the Unitarian Youth

Commission, which was to focus largely on the "college centers" dimension of youth programming. Its membership included representatives from the AUA, the Layman's League, the Ministerial Union, the YPRU, the Universalist General Convention, and the YPCU. The commission hired Stephen Fritchman full-time as director of youth activities.

Fritchman had received continental recognition in *The Christian Register* for his success with the youth group in the Unitarian church in Bangor, Maine, where he had been minister. In 1937, Frederick May Eliot, as newly elected president of the American Unitarian Association, had appointed Fritchman advisor to the YPRU. As the first outside "professional" ever associated with the YPRU and the first staff person not hired directly by the YPRU leadership, Fritchman soon won the trust of the youth leadership as well as the AUA administration. In his YPRU advisory capacity, Fritchman wrote one of the best handbooks on youth programming ever published for denominational use, *Young People in the Liberal Church.*

Both the denomination and the young people themselves recognized problems within the YPRU's organization at this time. The old structure was no longer adequate to serve present needs or develop new programs.

Since those on the forty-one-member YPRU Board of Directors who lived outside New England could rarely attend meetings because of costs and distances involved, the board usually met at one-third strength. Board members were elected for three-year terms and could serve as long as nine years. As a result, older, New England-based college students tended to run the organization.

In his 1942 report accompanying the re-organization plan, Stephen Fritchman pointed out the consequences of this antiquated structure:

> Because the YPRU organization as at present constituted cannot effectively reach its membership or its potential membership in any helpful way of service to a degree approaching success and efficiency, I must report that in my observation

the average church, even in Boston and New England, has ceased to give any deep loyalty or concern to the national organization. Because of a failure to serve its constituency, the organization has lost prestige and respect.

The organization failed to reach out to people outside of New England, and even people within a day's journey from Boston saw the YPRU's procedures as undemocratic and inadequate.

The YPRU leadership was not blind to these difficulties. However, dissatisfaction was stronger in the Midwest, which had a weaker regional organization than that of New England despite a strong base of local groups. In 1939, G. Richard Kuch (pronounced "Cook"), a Midwestern YPRU member attending Meadville Theological School, attempted to unite the Midwest groups in regional conferences. For sixteen years, since 1923, Star Island had been the site of the YPRU annual meeting. Youth had no conferences to compare with it outside of New England. Kuch, Paul Henniges and others organized a conference in the summer of 1940 at Lake Geneva, Wisconsin.

Kuch, vice president for the Midwest region, and Henniges, editor of the YPRU News, hitchhiked and leafleted the Midwest drumming up support for the Lake Geneva conference and for a stronger voice in the YPRU's national affairs. The YPRU's structural problems were also discussed at regional conferences in Manitoba, Canada, and Ardmore, Oklahoma. After this two-year buildup of strength, Kuch was a shoo-in for the YPRU presidency in 1941. His election represented a shift in the organization's geographic center of gravity.

Also in 1941, at Fritchman's urging, the YPRU created a Planning and Review Commission to survey the existing organization and to recommend changes. That commission, although based on an AUA model recommended by the Commission of Appraisal, proved ineffective.

Finally, the YPRU called a special board meeting for February 23-25, 1942, at the Senexet Pines Retreat near Woodstock, Connecticut. With twenty-three YPRU directors attending from Oklahoma,

Illinois, Missouri, and Eastern Canada, the two-day meeting had unprecedented representation, especially for wartime.

A "Committee of Four" was appointed at the Woodstock meeting to organize findings and make a final recommendation for the details of a re-organization. This group, all from the YPRU Executive Committee, included Dick Kuch, Robert Scott, Silas Bacon, and Barbara Hildreth. Within two weeks, the Committee of Four produced a draft of new purposes and by-laws for the YPRU, including a name change.

The committee first proposed the name "Unitarian Youth Fellowship," but encountered dissension in the ranks about whether to include the word *Unitarian*. More significant challenges addressed by the Committee of Four included the YPRU's undemocratic structure, the morass of red tape that seemed to occupy the headquarters' bureaucracy (and reinforce its remoteness from the local groups), and the lack of professional-quality field work.

That spring, the Committee of Four printed a series of preliminary recommendations. It suggested amalgamating high school and college work under one budget, with a professional and youth staff tied in with the AUA Department of Education. Internally, the committee recommended reducing the YPRU board's size and adopting more democratic procedures in the election of officers.

Following months of discussions, votes, and revisions, in a special meeting on October 17, 1942, in the AUA headquarters at 25 Beacon Street in Boston, Massachusetts, over one hundred YPRU delegates voted on the revised plan for re-organization.

This body voted to change the name of the YPRU to "American Unitarian Youth," set its age boundaries at fifteen to twenty-five years, bring school and college-age work under one budget, and limit the new AUY board to fourteen representatives designated by regions. Each regional representative was to be conscious of the interests of both high school- and college-age young people and represent from one to three federations. A four-member Executive Committee, elected by popular vote at biennial conventions, would preside over this new board.

A major policy change adopted in the re-organization was that board members would now have their expenses paid to attend board meetings, resulting in the final elimination of inbred New England leadership in the youth movement. American Unitarian Youth was on its way to becoming a truly continental organization.

In his essay covering this period of AUY history, Christopher Raible points out four important aspects of the re-organization: The process took place in wartime, many people of YPRU age faced the draft, travel was regulated by a government priority system, and little money was available for travel or institutional innovations. The fact that the AUY came into being at all under these circumstances is remarkable.

The move to lower and constitutionally fix the age of AUY members at fifteen to twenty-five involved a significant change in the character of the organizational leadership. Although college-age people would still be elected to continental offices, regional and local groups would tend to choose younger leaders. The change may also have increased the influence of the adult advisor, and later of the executive director, who would be associated with the AUY.

Encouraged by the opportunity for regular representation and power in the continental organization, regional groups within AUY began to emerge. This was the beginning of the regionalism that would come to dominate the later organization, Liberal Religious Youth (LRY), during the 1950s and 1960s.

Arnold Westwood took over the AUY presidency in 1943, as Kuch finished seminary and was called to a parish ministry in Illinois. Fritchman became director of American Unitarian Youth under the re-organization, working full-time at 25 Beacon Street. Then, in January, 1943, the AUA took over *The Christian Register*, and appointed Fritchman editor. His work with AUY, which reverted to part-time, was to be consumed by controversy after the end of the war.

The Universalist Youth Fellowship

Developments in the YPCU parallelled those in the Unitarian youth group. YPCU declined during the Depression but recovered somewhat in the later 1930s. Rev. Fenwick Leavitt, president from 1939 to 1941, reported that the number of local unions affiliated directly with the YPCU had increased from 97 to 134 between 1934 and 1939. Counting all the youth groups in Universalist churches, including those unaffiliated with the YPCU, brought the total to 230, the figure the YPCU normally reported. In 1939, the YPCU celebrated its fiftieth anniversary with much fanfare and the publication of a history of the Union, compiled and written by Rev. Harry Adams Hersey.

The problems of this time competed with the mood of celebration, however. The organization of the YPCU had always leaned strongly in favor of "states' rights." State unions held a great deal of power and were in competition with the national body for funds and energy. The cumbersome central YPCU structure consisted of a large council and an executive committee. The state unions paid the national body a blanket figure in dues each year. This was supposed to cover about half of the YPCU's budget, with the rest coming from the Universalist General Convention's Unified Appeal. Dues had become a source of tension within the organization; they usually weren't enough from the national point of view and always too much in the eyes of the state unions.

The denomination was applying pressure on the YPCU to change its mode of operation. The UGC, aware of the YCPU's internal controversies over finances, expressed concern about their effect on programming. UGC leaders also worried about the consequences of the YPCU's drop in the age range and the younger people coming into positions of leadership. Lacking a formal "Department of Young People," the denomination wanted the YPCU's programming tied more closely with the institutional church and its goals.

Like the Unitarian youth group, the Universalist youth movement undertook a major re-organization in response to internal and external pressures in 1941 and 1942. The Universalist restructuring, however, had more to do with financial and political arrangements with the Universalist General Convention, which was undergoing its own re-organization, marked by a name change to the "Universalist Church of America" (UCA). The Unitarian re-structuring represented the beginning of a different kind of youth group, one that was more truly continental in scope.

As with the Unitarians, the Universalist re-organization was primarily the work of a small group of leaders: Fenwick Leavitt, William Gardner, and Douglas Frazier were the architects. At the small 1941 YPCU convention in Oak Park, Illinois, they proposed a number of structural changes. Only sixty-two people, including forty-seven accredited delegates, attended, representing only nine states and twenty-one local unions.

The delegates renamed the organization "the Universalist Youth Fellowship" (UYF) and set its official age range at thirteen to twenty-five years. The organization could no longer appeal directly to the state unions and local groups for funds but would use its investment income (from holdings placed in trust by the UCA) and receive the remainder of its budget out of the UCA Unified Appeal.

In the Universalist Youth Fellowship's first year, the group elected Dana Klotzle president and Raymond Hopkins vice president. The UCA appointed Douglas Frazier as director of youth activities with part-time responsibilities for UYF. The Committee on Re-Organization by-laws describe the director's relationship to UYF as follows:

> The Director is appointed by the UCA with the approval of the corporation. The Director is the professional advisor to the corporation. She or he is in essence the "legal advisor or counsel" of the corporation.

The UYF, while gaining an "advisor," lost its full-time secretarial help through this reorganization.

The UCA also set up a Committee on Youth Activities consisting of two UYF representatives, one UCA board member, the UCA superintendent, the director of the Department of

Education, and the director of youth activities. The committee membership reflected a recommended structure in which voting adults would always exceed youth, ideally with a two-to-one ratio.

The War Years

The new Universalist organization and staff began on a hopeful note. A $4,400 bequest had pulled the YPCU out of debt for the first time in several years, so the Universalist Youth Fellowship began 1941-1942 with a balanced budget of $6,166. The leaders of UYF were usually students from Tufts college who were preparing for the Universalist ministry. However, when the war began, UYF saw many of its up-and-coming leaders drafted and faced increasing struggles for money and transportation to conferences.

The programs published by the UYF headquarters at this time reflected improvements in style and content. A 1942 UYF handbook consisted of separate loose-leaf booklets covering the whole spectrum of leadership training and programming for local groups. The programs it suggested remained largely worship or civic-oriented, with titles including "The American Way," "Understanding Ourselves," and "The Church and Its Faith."

Yet these national programs could not halt the decline in participation caused by the war. The draft was not the only problem. Even young civilians were mobilized to help the war effort in one way or another and had little spare time. National UYF leadership and programming became mostly office functions. Work with students reached a complete standstill. By 1943-1944, the UYF budget had been cut nearly in half, to $3,300.

In 1943, with Ann Postma succeeding Kotzle as UYF president, the Legion of the Cross for missions underwent a revival. With a great flourish, a New Church Building Fund was inaugurated for the purpose of building a church in memory of William Wesley Cromie, a young ministerial student who had died in an accident. In the late 1940s, when the fund had only reached $1,000 of its $6,000 goal, the proceeds were donated to the Association of Universalist Women for a chapel to be built at the Elliot Joslyn Home for Diabetic Boys. Small Legion of the Cross donations also went to the International Religious Fellowship and domestic field work.

In the fall of 1944, Douglas Frazier left the position of director of youth activities and was replaced by Roger Bosworth. During that year, the national office published a very thorough procedures guide for UYF local groups, prepared by old and new UYF leadership. It provided an excellent step-by-step outline of the problems and methods involved in leadership on all levels of a youth group's operation.

The UYF and AUY remained in close touch and co-operation with each other after their reorganizations and throughout the war, regularly exchanging delegates to each other's conventions and board meetings. A merger of the two groups remained under consideration.

As the war came to a close, the groups co-operated in publishing two small magazine-sized digests. *Youth for Action* focused entirely on social service. *The Young Liberal*, a more ambitious publication, was established in 1945 to be the main membership periodical for both groups.

Neither organization came out of the war years in a strong position. However, as the soldiers returned from Europe and the Pacific and the younger people in AUY-UYF knew peace for the first time since childhood, a mood of hope and excitement about the future prevailed.

It was during my high school days, 1938 to 1941, that I was a member of the YPCU of the First Universalist Church of Lynn, Massachusetts.

My family was active in the smaller Universalist Church in Swampscott, the adjacent town, where I had been attending church school with years of perfect attendance. However, as is often the case in the smaller churches, I was alone in my age group; and I did live in Lynn. My school chums and their older brothers and sisters were active in the Lynn church youth group. Thus it was a rather natural development for me to join. The first year I continued to go to Swampscott Sunday mornings and to Lynn Sunday evenings for YPCU; but then transferred all of my participation and membership to the Lynn Church.

The year 1938-1939 was the fiftieth anniversary of the founding of the YPCU, and its origin was in the Lynn Church. My impression of joining that fall was the experience of joy and celebration that the membership of the group had reached fifty—a goal set in recognition of the fiftieth anniversary. Another impressive memory is that it was my introduction to Gordon McKeeman, who was president (we married six years later and "lived happily ever after!"). Alice Harrison was our Advisor and also the director of religious education of the church.

We met weekly on Sunday evening and had programs and activities carefully planned by committees. Planning was done well in advance, in detail for three-month intervals, with annual events projected; sometimes topics were for a series of meetings. Each meeting had a worship service led by a member of the group and coordinated with the topic of the evening; a serious program, presentation, speaker, film, or whatever; recreation/games; and refreshments. We met at the church for two hours, probably between 6:00 and 8:00 p.m.; and there was always "the crowd" which adjourned to someone's home for a "post-mortem." We regularly scheduled joint events with the youth from the Jewish synagogue and from the black church. There was a range of special events, other than Sunday evening meetings, and group participation was emphasized and popular, even though there were a few "couples."

Some of the members also attended the high school class on Sunday morning—a part of the church school program. The class met earlier than other age groups so those who wished to could also attend the church service. There was rather a typical distribution of the YPCU group, maybe a third in the high school class, maybe a quarter or less in the church service. Also typical was the distribution of those whose families belonged to the church and those whose families were of other churches or unchurched.

The Lynn YPCU was active in the North Shore League with YPCU groups from the geographic area north of Boston and in the Massachusetts-Rhode Island YPCU. There were regularly scheduled conferences and annual events. Fall, winter, and spring rallies, the October climb up Mt. Monadnock, and occasional dances all drew attendance from multiple groups. Summertime always meant a week at Ferry Beach and Labor Day weekend was a special conference for the post-high school age.

Something to remember in the context of the late 1930s and early 1940s is that while the YPCU age range started with the high school age, the upper range was rather open-ended. Only some of the young people went away to college; others became employed or commuted to nearby colleges. Thus it was often the post-high school age people who were elected the top leaders of the groups, with the high school-age folk serving effective apprenticeships on active committees, etc. The World War II draft of young men introduced a drastic change, which then began to set the upper age limit at high school age. In Lynn, by 1942 we had a young adult group for the post-high school age with mostly a female membership. A major activity was a regular mimeographed newsletter to those away, especially those in military service, and meetings were continued so as to welcome any who visited home; reunions were popular.

I know that I was serving as secretary of the Massachusetts-Rhode Island YPCU when I was nineteen; when I was twenty or twenty-one and on the national board, I was chairman of the Junior High Committee. I have resisted name-dropping, but we continue to be in touch with a number of people we met through YPCU contacts, and indeed a goodly number have been and are prominent in UU affairs.

Phyllis McKeeman
Lynn, Massachusetts

Thirty-five years ago there were weekly Sunday night meetings of young people, ranging in age from fourteen to twenty, at the West Somerville Universalist Church in Massachusetts. Programs often featured a guest speaker; a discussion about the next picnic; plans for a roller skating party; gathering together to attend the Middlesex League of the Universalist Youth Fellowship; a special visit to a Universalist Church beyond the area of the aforesaid Middlesex League; a ten-minute devotional service led by one of the members; plans for a Youth Sunday program to be presented at the Sunday morning worship; songs around the piano—sacred as well as secular and "pop"; game periods featuring items found in most recreational handbooks, similar to those we had learned at Girl Scouts or Boy Scouts; and perhaps a pancake supper prepared by parents and/or the minister.

One of our ministers was very strong in the conscientious objector movement and brought in theologian friends from neighboring Tufts College (not yet a university) to explain why conscientious objectors were doing more to defend their country than those who bore arms. This minister also laughed easily, and his young wife seemed to enjoy the onslaught of loud teenagers at their tiny apartment as well as at the church meetings. He was run out of the church by the ruling elders for preaching sermons against war.

A few of the items discussed overtly by the members before, during, and after meetings included: How late did you stay out Saturday night? How tiring is it to be up until two o'clock after the movies and a visit to the dairy bar and a few kisses on someone's front porch and then have to revive on Sunday morning to attend Sunday School? Is it more funny to drop a button into the UYF offering plate, together with your nickel donation, or a metal slug? Why does Susie, presumably out of earshot on the other side of the room, suddenly seem to be dressing herself like a movie starlet when she doesn't have the figure for that kind of thing and just looks silly with four inches of makeup? Is smoking a good idea? Some of the most avid smokers thought it was fun to blow smoke though a handkerchief, leaving a nicotine stain. Should we take the Bible seriously, as our Baptist friends do, and do they really take it seriously? And how smart are we to be able to dance in church? How unfortunate are the Methodists that they can't? And why do Catholics believe in having so many children? And how come some of our Catholic friends are in one-, two-, or three-children families?

One night, when one of the conscientious objector theologians, from Crane Theological School at Tufts, came to our meeting, the question of the hour was whether fighting the Germans was similar to protecting our neighborhood and the virtue of neighborhood women from a maniacal gunman. Opinions were heated, but the patriots were worsted by the pacifists. The discussion continued on the walk home, but here the patriots got the upper hand and without violence. Most of the boys, who outnumbered the girls by two to one in this youth fellowship were drafted or enlisted within a year following Pearl Harbor.

The gathering of war clouds before and after Pearl Harbor produced a clear sense that all was not right in the world. Still, even the shock of Pearl Harbor did not diminish a sense that anything Americans wanted was right. Having struggled out of the Great Depression, America could do probably what it wanted to do.

So, what does it all add up to? The Sunday night meetings, which were so central and time consuming for a brief, intense time of growing up might seem to have vanished. For one of the members, these adolescent evenings still cast a spell. They offered a chance to socialize. They also encouraged the sharing of ideas not readily discussed in the public school, sorority, or fraternity. The meetings were a valid excuse to parents, if not teachers, to postpone high school homework. There was aesthetic stimulation through poetry, music, and candles lit sometimes in a youth-led vesper service, which were described as "this little liberal light of mine." To some of the members, these meetings were an escape from the authority of home, and school. To others they may have symbolized a contact with some kind of ideal for living. To all, they were an opportunity to celebrate the fact of being young, the youthful, emerging confidence.

Two of the twenty-five have offered, as this item is written, a total of forty-three years of professional leadership to a total of eight Unitarian and Universalist churches. One served as board member to the Universalist Publishing House. Another married a researcher *of programmed education and moved to California. Another has served on the official boards of two New England churches. If what one recalls of a third of these twenty-five may be representative of the whole, this tiny assemblage of youth and energy may still be unfolding, nurturing, producing.*

Robert H. MacPherson
West Somerville, Massachusetts

My memories of AUY always go back to Hnausa Camp on Lake Winnipeg, eighty-five miles north of Winnipeg in the early 1940s. The week there every summer was the highlight of the year's activities for our young people's group. What I remember most is getting up on the last morning to watch the sunrise over the lake, the baseball tournaments, the companionship, and getting to know the several wonderful people who came from afar to act as our advisors. The two that I remember particularly were Ernest Kuebler and Dick Kuch, who I still think of with fondness. We always had a wonderful week of sun, swimming, good food, plus some very good talks from our guests.

The highlight of my AUY days was a trip to Cleveland, Ohio, to a board meeting of AUY. It was the first time any Canadians were involved. I represented Western Canada, and Leslie McMahon of Ottawa represented Eastern Canada. This was my first time away from home alone, and today I am amazed my parents let me go. I had to change trains in Minneapolis and also in Chicago, so I can understand why they worried. When in Cleveland, I stayed with some wonderful people who had asked for the Canadian girls as they thought I might know their son-in-law stationed in with the Air Force in Vancouver (only about 1,500 miles from Winnipeg!). It appalled me to discover how little Americans knew of Canada.

Dick Kuch was vice president. As I had met him at Hnausa, I was glad to see a familiar face. I still remember how nice he was to me and how he showed me around the Field Museum in Chicago on the way home. The actual meetings in Cleveland are only a blur, as they were over thirty years ago.

I have only good memories of AUY and found the experience very rewarding.

Lilia Johnson Arnason
Winnipeg, Canada

Internationalism and the Cold War

THE DECADE AFTER the close of World War II was one of the most turbulent in the history of the Unitarian and Universalist youth movements. Ideological struggles over the church's relationship to communism rocked both the AUY and the UYF, as well as their affiliated denominations.

The World Youth Conference

The international political climate after World War II had a major impact on youth in the liberal religious movement. The Allies had liberated Europe and saved the world from Nazism, with the Soviet Union a wartime friend. Throughout the 1930s, the Unitarian and Universalist churches had attracted members and ministers from both the political left and the center, including sympathizers and supporters of the Soviet experiment and others who strongly opposed it.

American churches and relief agencies turned their attention to relief for the devastated countries of Europe. Unitarian and Universalist church journals and issues of AUY–UYF's publication *The Young Liberal* from 1945 through 1947 contain regular appeals to feed starving Czech and Dutch people and photographs of students helping to rebuild Stalingrad. Under the editorial leadership of Stephen Fritchman, *The Christian Register* also included intense editorials, articles, and debates about foreign policy issues.

Following the sacrifices of war, these years were marked by widespread international consciousness and heightened awareness of the fragility and significance of democracy in the world. AUY and UYF leaders who had passed their adolescence as civilians in wartime had seldom experienced international contact or travel. The last International Religious Fellowship conference on American soil had been in 1936. During the war, emergency committees had been created both in England and America to continue the work and to keep IRF alive. They had maintained a publication called *Forward*, but of course, with continental European participation impossible, IRF could hardly be the same as it once was.

Shortly after the war, plans for a World Youth Conference were announced. The conference was described as an opportunity to bring the world's youth together into a peacetime movement. Although not directly involved institutionally with organizing or planning the World Youth Conference, the AUY was somewhat connected to the event through the political views and connections of its staff. Also, AUY had an affiliation with the American Youth for a Free World, an anti-fascist youth organization, through Stephen Fritchman's past involvement. Martha Fletcher, an associate director of AUY and Fritchman's administrative assistant, was in charge of the U.S. Arrangements Committee for the World Youth Conference.

At the conference, held in London in November, 1945, Betty Green, the AUY president succeeding Arnold Westwood, and Ann Postma, the UYF president, attended as observers for their organizations. Green, of Leominster, Massachusetts, was the AUY's youngest president to date and the first woman ever to hold the office.

The two women were among more than six hundred delegates attending from sixty-two countries, representing an average age of twenty-seven. The North American youth groups had only received notice of the conference in July of that year, so the event was dominated by larger contingents from youth organizations in Europe—especially from socialist and communist countries.

Both Green and Postma traveled in Europe after the conference, including a trip to the Soviet Union in their itinerary. It was a tremendous experience for both. At that time, crossing the Atlantic meant a twenty-hour plane flight or several days on a boat. North Americans relied on print, radio, and newsreel journalism for information about the state of post-war Europe. Both Green and Postma sent back a running commentary about their travels, which was published in *The Young Liberal*. Following their return, the Universalist Church sent Postma on a national speaking tour to bring the world youth movement's message to churches and other groups.

Innuendo and Accusation

Despite tensions between communist and noncommunist groups at the World Youth Conference, both Green and Postma came back with extremely favorable reports about the new world youth organization, the World Federation of Democratic Youth (WFDY, pronounced "Woof-dee"). At its 1946 annual convention at Lake Geneva, Wisconsin, the AUY voted to affiliate with the WFDY. The UYF followed suit later that year.

By that time, the House Committee on Un-American Activities of the United States Congress was investigating alleged communist influence in American life. In testimony before the committee, the celebrated double agent Herbert Philbrick (author of *I Led Three Lives*) described communist organizing among the clergy and churches in Boston. He later claimed that he had not expected the testimony to become public. When it did, the names of Stephen Fritchman and Martha Fletcher were included among those Philbrick singled out as communist sympathizers and organizers. In fact, he named Fletcher as the head of the communist cell to which he himself had belonged. The accusations were based on flimsy evidence and innuendo, and nothing came of them beyond adverse publicity, which heated up when Fritchman was called to testify before the House Committee on Un-American Activities.

In the fall of 1945, Fritchman persuaded Dick Kuch to return to AUY from his parish ministry and take up the position of associate director. Kuch began work on January 1, 1946.

During Fritchman's and Kuch's leadership during the immediate postwar years, their political activism influenced a number of individual AUY members . On January 24, 1946, a picket line of clergy received national publicity for its support of the striking union at the General Electric Plant in East Boston. Picketers included Fritchman, Kuch, and Green. AUA President Frederick Eliot, upset by the publicity, called Fritchman and Kuch on the carpet for their involvement. Critics charged the two with leading impressionable young people into activities they did not understand and alleged that their actions were influenced or led by communist sympathizers. Kuch responded to this charge decades later in a 1971 interview with Rev. Philip Zwerling:

> We saw the picketing as simply putting good words about justice and equality to work. It's true that I did have a hell of a hold on the kids. I tried to use that popularity intelligently. We never painted the picture that over there was all good and over here was all evil. . . .
>
> Betty Green came out of a conservative environment in Leominster, Massachusetts, and once she'd seen the larger world, you couldn't have kept her back from doing the things she wanted to do.

International Initiatives and Stateside Conflicts

Kuch assumed a strong role in encouraging the international interest and spirit within the AUY, and, through the pages of *The Young Liberal*, in the UYF as well. In the summer of 1946, he sat in on the WFDY Council meeting in Paris and visited the Unitarian congregation in Prague.

Kuch also reported on the gathering at Flagg, near Manchester, England, which had convened to reorganize the International Religious Fellowship. No official American delegates attended the conference, where international representation was otherwise very broad. Delegates represented Australia, Austria, Belgium, Czechoslovakia, Denmark, England, Ireland, France, Germany, Holland, Hungary, and Switzerland.

The group revised the IRF constitution to meet the needs of a new era and new generation of IRF members and elected a general secretary. Delegates adopted resolutions expressing good will toward liberal German youth and liberal religious prisoners of war. This meeting was written up in *The Young Liberal*, and the American groups volunteered to print the IRF publication, *Forward Together*, in a quarterly supplement to *The Young Liberal* as their contribution to the IRF. Meeting in their respective 1946 conventions, AUY and UYF each voted to sponsor at least one delegate to the 1947 IRF conference in Switzerland.

American Unitarian Youth further accredited Jean Casson as its official delegate to another large international gathering, the International Student Congress in Prague, where the International Union of Students was founded. Casson wrote to Kuch that he observed political tension within the American delegation over conference issues. He saw danger of the delegation splitting along ideological lines.

Postwar international youth activity moved toward a climax when plans were announced for a World Youth Festival to be held in Prague from July 20 to August 17, 1947. Invitations went to governments and youth groups the world over. A number of different youth organizations, including the WFDY, were involved in the planning, though the communist and socialist countries undertook the lion's share.

From 1946 to 1947, the AUY made plans for a new international program of its own. During the five years that the United States had fought in World War II, the AUY had sponsored summer work camps in different parts of the U.S. and Canada. Combining public service and work with a summer holiday in an AUY conference atmosphere, these camps had played a valuable part in maintaining and vitalizing the continental thrust of the

AUY represented by the 1941 reorganization. Camps were held in New England, of course, but also in places like Manitoba in Western Canada, bringing the AUY groups there in closer touch with their counterparts from other parts of the continent.

After the war, the AUY decided to sponsor a work camp in Czechoslovakia. The group contacted the Czech Unitarians and government and publicized the event. The summer of 1947 was to be an important summer abroad. As the year began, however, AUY was experiencing an internal political crisis.

Since the end of the war, Stephen Fritchman had come under considerable attack within the Unitarian denomination for his personal political views and his style in editing The Christian Register. Critics of Fritchman's politics and activities included some AUY members. As early as December, 1945, a letter was published in The Christian Register from AUY leader Charles M. Sherover. The letter attacked "the apparent political line of the Register Editor who must insist on consistently identifying the various communist groups in foreign countries as the democratic forces, and who sees in the foreign policy of the Soviet Union the one and only hope and guiding star of democratic freedom and progress."

Many of Fritchman's critics were also concerned about his influence on young minds. In a letter to Eliot on October 24, 1946, Rev. A. Powell Davies of the All Souls' Church of Washington, D.C., wrote that the youth group of his church would henceforth be "only nominally affiliated" with the AUY as long as Fritchman remained director.

The Board of Directors of the American Unitarian Association expressed support of Fritchman's editorship when it considered his work in a meeting on October 9, 1946. However, the board referred accusations of Fritchman's communist sympathies to the director of the Department of Publications and Education. In January, 1947, Fritchman offered his resignation as advisor to American Unitarian Youth, effective February 15. Eliot's report to the AUA board on the resignation implied that Fritchman had resigned as a result of the conclusions reached by the director of the Department of Publications and Education.

Fritchman would have this to say, in a 1973 letter to Phillip Zwerling:

> The reason I resigned as a youth worker was that I was tired after eight years of a job which I had done, and felt had been completed . . . . Also, the Register had become a very demanding full-time job.

In the spring of 1947, Fritchman resigned as editor of *The Christian Register* rather than submit his editorial copy to the AUA administration for approval. However, he withdrew his resignation after deciding to take his case to the people of the denomination at the 1947 May Meetings. The May Meeting delegates voted with the administration, and Stephen Fritchman left 25 Beacon Street.

As the American Unitarian Association's first professional youth worker, Fritchman represented the beginning of adult denominational involvement in the Unitarian youth organization. His role in recognizing the inadequacies of the old Young People's Religious Union, while bringing together the new American Unitarian Youth, marked a milestone in the history of the movement. He was fortunate in having a cadre of very talented YPRU and AUY leaders working with him to make that reorganization effective. Fritchman's leadership and insight on the printed page and in the field attracted respect for "youth work" in the American Unitarian Association, as well as controversy.

Kuch stayed on as Associate Director of AUY for another year after Fritchman's resignation, in effect serving as acting director. Within AUY concern was growing about the direction the World Federation of Democratic Youth was taking. A constitutional convention was planned, with an agenda that would include thrashing out some of the differences over the organization's political stance.

In January of 1947, Kuch went to Europe to meet with WFDY and IRF officials and further the plans for the Czech work camps. Upon his return, he wrote the only direct retort concerning the communist scare and the AUY to appear in *The Young Liberal.* In the March-April 1947 issue, Kuch described the concerns he had heard expressed concerning the influence of communism on the young AUY members planning to go to Eastern Europe. Kuch's reply was that with more practical "training in democracy," through the youth movement and within the church, youth would be even better prepared to justify and defend the democratic system.

This did little to quiet the criticism, now focused on the Czech work camp project. On May 27, 1947, Kuch received a telegram from the National Committee of Free Unitarians (a lay group that had organized against Fritchman and other "communist" influences within the AUA), protesting "The intention of American Unitarian Youth to send thirty Unitarian students to communist-dominated Czechoslovakia for six weeks this summer for amateur brick laying which takes three years to learn . . . . We respectfully suggest that the total of $4,550.00 involved be donated to relieve suffering in Great Britain, France, and other democratic countries."

The delegation that went to Europe in 1947 was led by the Reverend Bob Zoerhide of Peterborough, New Hampshire, and David Parke, who at age eighteen had succeeded Betty Green as AUY president. At its first stop—the work camp in Hradec, Czechoslovakia, some twenty-seven American and eighty Czechoslovakian Unitarian youth worked together mining coal, fighting the spread of a disease affecting trees in the area, and rebuilding the village of Balaze, which had been destroyed in the war.

Then a group of AUY members went to Prague for the World Youth Festival. That mammoth event, with 25,000 participants from 22 countries, included sports, concerts, displays, and other cultural activities.

The American delegation seemed weak and ill-organized, largely because at the last minute, the U.S. State Department had denied a previously-granted request for transportation for up to five hundred delegates on two C-4 transport ships.

The State Department's claim was that it could only offer that kind of support to nonpolitical groups. Consequently, such "po-

litical" groups as the Yale University basketball team couldn't make
it to Prague. As a result, the Festival was dominated by large contingents from the Eastern European countries, particularly the
Soviet Union, where the definition of "youth" included people as
old as thirty-five. Nevertheless, during their week in Prague, the
AUY members performed a presentation of "Songs of America"
before nearly a thousand delegates.

In a culmination of three events, overlapping in a three-week
period, the work camp and World Youth Festival were followed by
the International Religious Fellowship conference, held at
Arcegno, Switzerland, from August 10 to 17, 1947. David Parke,
Carl Beck, and Wendell Lipscomb served as official AUY delegates
to IRF. Kuch, coming directly from the Czech work camp, attended the conference as an observer.

Later, reporting the IRF conference in AUY publications, Kuch
described its beginning days as a series of speeches in the morning
and a series of speeches in the afternoon. He called these theme
talks dull and disorganized. The Americans had come from AUY's
1947 annual convention at Star Island with some definite proposals for a new IRF. The Americans were as much to blame as anyone for a lackluster year for IRF. They had failed to publish a single
issue of *Forward Together*. The Swiss finally decided to take on that
responsibility. Now, after a disorganized year, this conference was
turning out to be a bore. A group of delegates decided to take action to remedy the situation.

The Americans joined forces with the British, as well as some
Dutch and Czechs, to propose transforming the conference, mid-
week, into a series of working commissions on various IRF problems. Commission topics covered organization, program, publications, membership, and extension.

Debate and politicking about a new IRF was spirited. The delegates voted to move the unofficial IRF "headquarters" from
Utrecht, Holland, to Prague, in recognition of the strong Czech
youth movement and as a gesture of support and hope for the
continued growth. The IRF adopted the "commission" approach

to doing business, reminiscent of "working groups" within boards, as a permanent feature. The American proposal to undertake the publication of *Forward Together* was renewed for 1947-1948 and accepted. Finally, the IRF initiated a program to contact religious liberals from outside the Christian tradition. The issue of their participation in IRF was never completely resolved, however, and would flare into a major controversy several years later.

In a battle over elections, many delegates felt that they should be allowed to nominate from the floor candidates who had not been suggested by the Executive Committee. When the electoral dust settled, Dick Kuch had been elected president of IRF, succeeding Karel Haspel of Czechoslovakia.

The WFDY Controversy

American Unitarian Youth's affiliation with the World Federation of Democratic Youth met with a challenge at the 1947 AUY convention. A committee on "Co-ordination with Other Youth Groups" was commissioned to draw up a complete report on WFDY and the pros and cons of affiliation. The committee's chairman was Charles Eddis, later to become an AUY president and a Unitarian minister.

The WFDY had never enjoyed the unanimous support of AUY members. A strong minority had opposed affiliation at the previous year's convention, citing WFDY's communist participants. Continentally, the political leanings of the AUY's adult leadership, the popular internationalism of the post-war period, and the personal experience of the AUY's youth leadership in Europe had pulled the AUY toward international youth movements that were left of center. That direction had not been taken without some dissent, however, and now, a new group of AUY leaders was coming into positions of power.

In 1948, the Co-ordination Committee presented a fifty-page report on the WFDY to the American Unitarian Youth annual meeting in Stillwater, Oklahoma. The report included a history of WFDY, an analysis of the political sympathies and affiliations of WFDY leadership, personal observations and reports from AUY members who were in London in 1945 and in Prague in 1947, and a fair list of the pros and cons of affiliation. On top of that, the committee had included a capsule summary of liberal and communist philosophies.

A last straw for many AUY leaders had been the purging of the only noncommunist member of WFDY's Secretariat. AUY wrote a letter condemning the move. By the time the affiliation question came to the 1948 annual meeting in Oklahoma for a vote, AUY, UYF, and the American Youth for a Free World were the only American affiliates WFDY had left.

Informal discussion centered on the issue throughout the week-long conference. Delegates had opportunities to read WFDY material and see a pro-WFDY film. Following a debate on the floor lasting one and a half hours, the convention voted to disaffiliate. AUY Council members Peter Raible, Leon Hopper, Kurt Hanslowe, and Louise Gartner were among those appointed to a committee for writing up a statement explaining the decision.

The Universalist Youth Fellowship took the same action later the same year. Its 1948 resolution of disaffiliation argued that the World Federation of Democratic Youth "has become primarily a political propaganda organization, with which the Universalist Youth Fellowship, being primarily a religious organization, has little in common."

The WFDY controversy within the AUY and UYF did not make a big splash on the local level. The debate laws focused largely among the continental and regional leaders over a two-year period. The Universalists, who held their conventions later in the year than the Unitarians, appeared to follow the latter's lead both in affiliating and disaffiliating from WFDY. However, due to lack of money, the Universalists did not, and could not, participate in the international activity to the same degree that the Unitarians could.

The furor surrounding Fritchman and the WFDY issue reflected a larger battle raging in the denomination and in society at large. The Unitarian Service Committee was caught up in a communist controversy of its own, and many churches and denominations were touched by the beginnings of what would develop into the witch hunts of the McCarthy era.

The international spirit of co-operation and friendship that instigated the controversy should not be dismissed because of the dissension that developed from it. Valuable connections were made during that time, most particularly with the revived International Religious Fellowship.

IRF on Firm Ground

The International Religious Fellowship continued to sputter along during the latter 1940s. From 1947 to 1948, the organization remained nearly as disorganized as it had been in 1946, despite the successful 1947 conference. Kuch simply could not put as much effort into IRF as was required, and his resignation from the AUY staff in mid-year came too late for AUY to find anyone else who could carry the ball. For the second year in a row, the Americans failed to print *Forward Together*. On top of that, with the new communist government of Czechoslovakia tightening travel restrictions on both Czechs and foreigners, the IRF Secretariat in Czechoslovakia would not function. Halfway through the year, it became apparent that the 1948 IRF conference could not be held in Czechoslovakia as planned.

The site was changed to Denmark, but the conference drew only ten people from outside that nation. The previously strong, Czech delegation could not obtain passports. Lawrence Jaffa and Charles Eddis attended from America. Eddis, designated as the AUY's official international delegate, spent that summer going to the conferences of AUY's remaining international affiliates.

The IRF ceremonially elected Ludek Benes, a Czech, as its new president, but the executive secretary, Brian Whitehead of England, assumed major responsibility for the coming year. Plans were laid for the 1949 conference to be held in Holland in conjunction with the International Association for Religious Freedom (IARF) Congress.

Eddis took his IRF responsibilities seriously over the following year. He assumed editorship of *Forward Together* and turned out good issues on time. An American IRF Committee was formed with AUY and UYF representatives, and in 1949 four AUY members attended the Holland conference. With an annual budget of about $3,000 and a stronger leadership core, IRF grew steadily more effective after 1949, achieving the continuity and stability necessary to hold together such a geographically diverse organization.

The international enthusiasm within our postwar youth movement allowed the International Religious Fellowship to transcend its European base and complete the process of including the North Americans within their fold, a process that had only just begun when it was interrupted by World War II.

Until 1939, the IRF was organized only through its headquarters in Holland, which kept in touch with the youth groups of the churches that were members of the IARF. Thus, in England, the Fellowship of Youth, the Young People's League, and a few individual members were in contact with Holland, but there was no English IRF committee. In 1940, after the invasion of Holland, Elspeth Hall (later Rev. E. Vallance) was mainly responsible for suggesting the setting up of an Emergency Committee in England to keep in touch with members in countries still free from Fascist domination. Joan Hartley (later Mrs. J. Haenisch of California) undertook the enormous job of contact secretary. Our chief aim was to keep the fellowship alive until it could function, as before, as an international body. To keep the IRF going here, we organized weekend conferences, produced duplicated issues of an English language Forward Together, *and spent many hours preparing an ambitious "Study Guide." We exchanged letters with members in America and were glad to hear that their activities increased as the Unitarian and Universalist youth groups worked more closely together.*

When I became secretary, I was handed a strong cardboard box, containing many small slips of thin paper with names and addresses of the members of the various national groups known to the Dutch at the outbreak of the war. I was told that if the Germans invaded Great Britain, the lists must be destroyed, as it would be dangerous to have international sympathies during a Nazi occupation. At Christmas, 1944, when I was away on a visit, a "flying bomb" landed on the house in Oldham, Lancaster, where I had "digs," and completely demolished it. Apparently it went through my bedroom, and if I had been there then I would not be here now! My landlady was badly injured and some of our neighbors killed. It was some days before I heard what had happened and returned to claim my possessions. The stuff that had been pulled out of the wreckage of several houses—furniture, clothes, curtains, carpets, cases, books, papers— wet and sometimes blood-stained—was piled up in dusty heaps in an old Sunday School, and friends helped me to rummage through it and find what was mine. I found a few odd shoes, a case of clothing, some of my books, but I realized that what really mattered was contacts. Clothes, I could make or borrow; furniture, replace; shoes were a problem at that stage of the war, and books, difficult—but the thing that I must find was that list! At last, someone popped up from behind a torn settee and held up the box, unopened and safe. "Is this what you're looking for?" That list was, in fact, our chief means of re-establishing communications after the war.

In the summer of 1945, when first Holland and then the rest of Europe was gradually and painfully freed, we began to receive and send letters and to hear of all that had been endured. We sent a letter to everyone on that list asking for information and spent all our spare time and many of our nights in replies. The people of Holland, especially those in the Arnhem area, were destitute. They were literally starving, having had only small and irregular rations during the occupation and been deprived of even the bicycles on which they used to travel long distances to buy food from the farm. Their houses were often ransacked by the German soldiers. Their young men had lived in hiding to avoid forced labor in Germany; many had been in concentration camps, and very many were ill. Yet the strange thing is that some Germans still believed that they were welcome in Holland.

We had a fine German Quaker Esperantist member in the camp in Leersum, Holland, in 1938. He had refused military service (brave man!) and had joined the Red Cross. When he was sent to Holland he wrote to an IRF member, who was also an Esperantist, to invite her to meet him. She was in a dilemma. Imagine what the Dutch would think of a girl who fraternized with a German! Nevertheless, she went—and found that he had no idea of the feeling that the invasion had aroused in Holland. I imagine that the meeting was brief, but at least it shows that the spirit of our fellowship could pass even that barrier.

The greatest joy in that year was to hear from the secretary of the IRF, Jeltje Vorster, and to start planning for the revival of the Fellowship internationally. We joined in a scheme to send Red Cross parcels of necessities to Dutch people in need and, optimistic as ever, we organized an "international" conference at Flagg, England, for the summer of 1945, but we could not persuade the authorities to give visas to visitors from abroad. In the December we issued the first Forward Together *printed after the war.*

Finally, in the summer of 1946 (in the week in which bread rationing started in Britain), we managed, with the help of that General Assembly, to hold a week's conference in Manchester, attended by several of our old, and some new, friends from Czechoslovakia, Holland, Denmark, Belgium, Switzerland, Austria, France, and Ireland. It was the most exciting week of my life! And now, "old" was the relevant word—for most of us had passed the magic age of thirty-five and we had to hand the Fellowship on to the younger ones. For me, the war really came to an end that week—but not the friendships we had formed, for we have carried them on into the IARF. There, we do not meet so often and our numbers are declining—but we have shared an experience that goes very deep and it has colored our outlook ever since, for to quote from one of the first letters we received from Holland, "It was a real help to know that there was in this dreadful time a fellowship, the members of which could not reach one another but who had the same belief and who . . . certainly would re-live the splendid hours we were together, work-

ing, talking, singing, and praying. Though separated, we felt bound together with them."

Lorna Davidson
Lancaster, England

We Would Be One

A VERY DYNAMIC GROUP of youth leaders and the domestic and international politics of the time make the postwar era a significant period in this history. Many of these leaders would go on to enter the ministry and serve Unitarian Universalist parishes. Their initiative and continuing work during this time brought the UU movement through the institutional changes leading to creation of Liberal Religious Youth.

The Hinsdale Meeting and Its Aftermath

People make the politics, and the leaders of the American Unitarian Youth in the late forties were a highly political group. David Parke succeeded Betty Green to the AUY presidency in June 1947, having come up through the Executive Committee ranks for three years. Then a freshman at Antioch College, Parke took the 1947-1948 year off from college to work full-time for AUY. In January 1947 his vice president, Charles Sherover, and Peter Raible had organized the Chicago Area Council of Liberal Religious Youth, a major center of influence in AUY west of Boston.

In his essay "A Short Subjective History of the Unitarian and Universalist Youth Movements," Leon Hopper points to organizational changes enacted at Hinsdale, Illinois, in December, 1947, as milestones on the road to the merged Universalist and Unitarian youth organization, Liberal Religious Youth (LRY). Hopper writes of the new relationship with the denomination that arose from this Hinsdale meeting, particularly in terms of how it promoted the idea of "youth autonomy" within AUY, and later, LRY:

> The present and future shape of [the youth organization] and of the Continental as we know it today was cast in a meeting in Hinsdale, Illinois, in December, 1947. Ernest Kuebler, Director of the AUA Department of Education, and Dr. Frederick May Eliot, President of the AUA, met with the American Unitarian Youth Council to discuss the future relationship of the AUY to the AUA, and that of AUY's professional staff to the Association.
>
> The AUA staff proposed a plan to the AUY Council: the Department of Education to hire a Director of Youth Activities to be paid by the Association and the AUY to hire and pay for its own staff from its own budget. (The AUY received funds from the United Unitarian Appeal.) The Council presented many reasons for rejecting this proposal, but in the end accepted it. And this was the beginning of "youth autonomy."

Hopper's picture of AUA pushing the AUY into a more autonomous position, almost against the latter's will, is true to a certain extent. Following Stephen Fritchman's resignation, the departure of senior staff member Kuch seemed inevitable. Controversy had continued to surround AUY's 1947 summer activities, both in Europe and in connection with the Star Island conference and annual meeting.

In its October 1947 report, the AUA's Commission on Planning and Review expressed satisfaction at the intensified "national activities" within the youth movement, but added certain reservations:

> Despite these commendable activities, summer institutes have not presented the various points of view representing the Unitarian outlook; there has often not been the accom-

panying development of the national program which has too
often been lacking on the part of large numbers of Unitarian
adults because of lack of information.

Kuch said that when the AUY Council met at Hinsdale, it
faced "Eliot and Kuebler and the boys all present explaining to us
how it was going to be." "How it was going to be" was as Hopper
described it: The AUA would continue to hire and pay for a director of youth education, who would function in the same staff capacity that Fritchman and Kuch had. Although Fritchman had
been hired by the AUA, all previous YPRU staff had been responsible only to the YPRU board, so their "autonomy" was an established fact prior to AUY's creation. Fritchman, though paid by the
AUA, had been hired in close consultation with YPRU leaders, and
of course, Kuch had come out of the ranks. At Hinsdale, the main
problem that the AUY leadership had with the AUA's proposal was
that Frederick Eliot had already decided on the person he wanted
to appoint to the new staff position that he was creating, without
any prior consultation with AUY.

Though AUY leaders reacted strongly against the idea of having a new staff person imposed upon them in this way, Eliot
would not budge. AUY decided to hire its own staff people and
pay them out of its own budget, above and beyond the director
hired by the AUA.

When the dust cleared and hirings had been completed in the
summer of 1948, Clifton Hoffman, Eliot's choice, had joined the
AUA staff as director of youth education, with a far wider scope of
responsibilities than AUY. Hoffman was a minister and former
dean of students at the University of Chicago's divinity school.
The AUY hired Paul Henniges, minister for the Unitarian Church
in Long Beach, California. Henniges, formerly editor of *The YPRU
News*, had been a friend of Kuch's during the reorganization.
David Parke notes that outside of the youth leaders, continuity in
the AUY office was maintained by office secretary Mildred
Saunders (later Vickers), who was a mainstay of stability and efficiency in the organization.

The AUY's "autonomy" within the AUA proved to be a mixed blessing. Financially, it became a real problem. After only two years, the AUA had to discontinue Hoffman's job due to lack of funds. In February 1950 Charles Eddis summarized the consequences of the new relationship:

> Two years ago AUY's net budget was a bit over $15,000. Today AUY has approximately the same budget, but there is one big difference. While two years ago the AUA supplied the AUY with a full-time staff of three, today AUY pays the salaries of its staff out of its own budget, thus reducing AUY's effective budget considerably. The AUY staff has been reduced, and the AUA staff in the youth field wiped out completely, with the absence of a Director of Youth Education and of secretarial staff under him.

In May of 1950, the United Unitarian Appeal reached only 55 percent of its goal. Everyone suffered as a result. The AUY received only $8,312 out of its anticipated $14,000 allocation. The organization had been functioning on a hand-to-mouth basis for some years. Each year, it had borrowed money in the hope that the United Appeal would come in with a little bit extra in May, which never happened. Beginning in 1948, Parke and Kuch had investigated the possibility of using endowment fund capital to regain financial stability. In its 1949 annual meeting, the AUY voted to remove $14,880 from endowment fund capital to meet debts and expenses. Given these circumstances, the consensus was to live within the limits of a $10,815 budget for 1950-1951. A full three-quarters of that budget went into staff salaries and office expenses. Midwinter council meetings had to be cancelled, and the AUY's continental publication, *The Young Liberal*, discontinued.

Success and Failure in College-Age Programming

Most of the programming that the liberal churches directed at college-age people before World War II happened at the local and regional levels, under the direction of such groups as the Boston Student Committee and individual college center ministers. The last systematic effort at large-scale college work had been the Student Federation of Religious Liberals back in the 1920s. The AUY had a "Student Work" Committee, which functioned on a small scale.

When the war ended, however, there was a pressing need for more to be done in this area. The reorganization had lowered the age of the leadership in both the AUY and the UYF. The continental leaders were now in their late teens or early twenties, usually in their early college years, while the age range of the local groups had lowered proportionately. Young people returning from military service found themselves older than the existing local group members, but still interested in the kind of programs and group experience that AUY and UYF provided.

The AUY Student Work Committee had made preliminary contacts with students on campuses, where Fritchman had devoted half of his AUY time to college work. AUY representatives identified several strong local centers, such as Berkeley, California; Chicago, Illinois; Urbana, Illinois; and Northampton, Massachusetts, where college-age seminars and conferences could succeed.

At the 1947 AUY conference on Star Island, the AUY Executive Committee and staff created a Channing Foundation to serve college-age people. With a $1,100 budget, a seven-person Channing Foundation Committee was set up in the Midwest to coordinate a national program, using regional committees as bases. The following summer, the Universalist Youth Fellowship formalized its student work under the title of the "Murray Foundation." Only $100 was allocated for expenses, so it appears correspondence was meant to be its major organizing tool. The two groups published a joint college-age magazine, *The Liberal's Challenge.*

Organizationally, neither program really got off the ground. Many people put a great deal of time into the effort, including the older AUY leaders such as Green, Sherover, and Raible, but a real continental program similar to AUY or UYF was an unreachable goal. Many local Channing Foundation chapters thrived, however.

In fact, from 1949 to 1951, the Tri-U group in Minneapolis assumed responsibility for coordinating the whole Continental Channing Foundation Committee (CCFC), but the minutes from that time report that the CCFC had "a pitiful existence."

June 1950 saw the outbreak of the Korean War and another mobilization of college-age people. The draft hurt the Murray Foundation program, which was smaller and less able to afford the loss of leaders, more than the Channing Foundation.

One reason the college efforts never succeeded is that many college-age leaders in both organizations were siphoned off into the regional and continental organizing of the high-school aspect of the program. Also, the regional organizations that formed the true base of the programs really succeeded only in the Midwest and New England.

Money, of course, was also a reason. The Universalists never could budget a serious sum toward college work, and the Unitarian effort was caught in a budget crunch as the 1940s ended.

Peter Raible, who did considerable work in the Midwest for the Channing Foundation, wrote a bitter memo in 1951 to Frank Ricker of the Pacific Central District blaming the failure of the program on the lack of any significant funds. He pointed out that when churches near campuses lend assistance, they receive no lasting benefit: the students eventually move away.

Local Channing and Murray groups often included non-campus college-age people. In 1948, thirty-four out of eighty-eight groups in the Channing Foundation directory fell into that category. Many individuals in these groups were not Unitarians. This appears to have been a bone of contention in some groups, as it has been more recently in some LRY and YRUU local groups. The 1948 Channing Foundations College Guide notes,

> The relation of the local group to the church also depends a good deal on the proportion of Unitarians or non-Unitarians in the group . . . in the heavily divided or almost completely non-Unitarian group, the relationship of the group to the church has a tendency to be confused and dif-

ficult. The big point to remember is that non-Unitarian religious liberals have usually had an unpleasant experience in another church and do not want to be pushed toward church membership in any way. . . . It is important, though, to make it clear that you are a Unitarian group. Many college groups de-emphasize this fact and make a great mistake. If we are really Unitarians, we should not hide that fact merely to appease a few potential members.

By 1951, as the merger process between the AUY and the UYF reached full swing, both the Channing and Murray Foundations seemed on their last legs. Older members increasingly looked upon the AUY and the UYF as high-school-aged organizations. In 1953, following the AUY-UYF merger, the programs would merge into the Channing-Murray Foundation and be completely re-evaluated.

The Postwar UYF

Without doubt, the most important development within the Universalist Youth Fellowship following World War II was the arrival on the scene of Alice Harrison. For over thirty years, her career in the liberal church centered around ministry to young people. Harrison's unique influence was felt most keenly in the area of junior high programming, but one of the things that made her presence in the youth program so important was her ability to relate to young people of all ages.

Harrison began her liberal religious education career at the Universalist Church in Lynn, Massachusetts. She served as an advisor in YPCU events on the local and regional levels, beginning in 1936. In 1945, the Universalist Church of America hired her as a staff member for religious education. When Roger Bosworth resigned in 1946, Harrison became the UCA's director of youth activities.

The Universalists had always been more inclusive of the junior high–age people in their youth group than the Unitarians. Harrison's presence as director of youth activities ensured that the UYF program would continue to include college-age, high school, and junior high people. The average age of YPCU membership had decreased more slowly than it had among the Unitarians; at the time Fenn Leavitt took over as the last YPCU president, he was in his early thirties. The change really happened from the bottom up. Because of the UYF's smaller size, and because the UYF membership was less politicized than that of AUY, leaders tended to progress gradually through the ranks from the local level as they showed interest and talent.

As previously noted, the UYF came out of the war years in a weakened condition. By 1947-1948, however, it was showing financial recovery, operating with a budget of about $5,000, not including Harrison's salary. UYF had to discontinue co-publication with the AUY of *The Young Liberal*, however. The magazine had increased in size and frequency from its original format, and its overall publication costs had doubled original expectations within a year. Delegates to the 1947 UYF annual meeting voted to discontinue the joint publication "purely for the purpose of strengthening our own organization." The major reason for the move was that the UYF could not hold up its end of the costs through subscriptions, which in early 1947 were running twenty to one below those from Unitarian subscriptions. For the money required, the Universalists had not been getting a publication that benefited them. They returned to printing their own journal, *The Youth Leader*.

Harrison's job required extensive travel to organize and visit groups for all three age levels of the UYF. The leadership and board remained centered in New England. The annual "New England Get-Together" conference each February often drew more people than the national convention. The "power blocs" within the UYF were based in state unions, with the most populous and well organized in New England, such as the Massachusetts-Rhode Island and Maine unions.

The UYF's changing character showed in a new set of purposes passed at the 1948 convention in Norway, Maine. These replaced an old paragraph in the constitution entitled "Objects," which read,

The object of this fellowship shall be: The promotion of Christian culture, service, and leadership among the young people of the Universalist Church and the extension of the power and influence of liberalism in every way possible.

The six concise new purposes passed at the 1948 meeting made no mention of the word *Christian* and contained no specific references to the Universalist Church. At the following year's meeting, a routine motion of greeting to the Universalist Church of America was amended upon the motion of Bill DeWolfe to eliminate the words "its parent organization."

A Different Style

An institutional narrative of this period cannot capture the un-mistakably changed style and atmosphere of the youth movement in the 1940s. In looking at those years, compared to previous decades, the feel of the movement becomes more familiar to those who have been involved with the LRY or YRUU in later times.

Youth leaders began to take time out from school to work full-time for the youth organizations. Field-tripping by the youth leadership via hitchhiking, rail, and soon air became common. In early 1948, David Parke spent two months on a long and thorough field trip down the West Coast of the United States and Canada. He arranged to meet Dick Kuch and his 1948 Hudson ("a gorgeous hunk of automobile") in Texas to drive back East.

Richard Woodman remembers well the travails of hitchhiking to New England UYF conferences: "It took me twenty-five rides to get from Boston to North Adams." In the minutes of the 1949 UYF convention, we find the following resolution:

Be it recommended that the UYF set up a commission which is to form an independent organization to be called Hitch-hikers International…which will have as its purpose the promotion of safe and speedy hitchhiking by whatever means it sees fit.

A well-publicized event of the summer of 1948 was the "AUY Caravan," reminiscent of the 1930s Peace Caravans. Having resolved to tour all the western AUY summer camps, Leon Hopper, Carl Beck, and their magnificent Crosley automobile completed that journey—chugged 2,600 miles from Tulsa, Oklahoma, to Seattle, Washington, back down to Asilomar in California, and finally returning to Beck's hometown of Pittsburgh. They averaged eight miles an hour over the Rockies, but the only major trouble they experienced was losing the fan belt right through the radiator on the way to Asilomar.

In 1949, after losing a closely contested presidential election to Chuck Eddis, Hopper decided to take time off from school anyway and become an official AUY field director.

The 1948 AUY convention in Stillwater, Oklahoma, represented a major change in AUY conference programming. It was the organization's first convention west of the Mississippi or south of the Mason-Dixon line. Because of distances, only one hundred delegates were able to attend (compared to three hundred the year before at Star Island). The AUY's first gathering in the South created a serious problem in the conference arrangements, for state law forbade blacks and whites to share sleeping quarters. The college hosting the conference was persuaded to bend its own segregation rules, but would not allow attendees to break state laws. AUY planners decided to hold the conference there regardless, so Mildred Saunders, the AUY office secretary—who had been the first black person working at the AUA in any position other than maintenance staff—was forced to sleep down the road in a motel.

The Stillwater gathering was also the first attempt at a week-long AUY convention. Being together for a week brought the summer camp experience and the AUY convention together. By that time, the conferences had started experiencing the types of rule issues that would emerge at later gatherings. Regulations around curfews and drinking were more explicit than in later years, however, and violations usually led to more severe action. Small controversies emerged around discussions of sexuality at Star Island in 1947 and about co-ed dorms at one of the Murray Grove conferences.

Part of the reason for adult concern about conferences, especially in the UYF, was the growing presence of more junior high-age youth. The age range at these conventions meant that attendees who were over twenty-one, a clear minority, had to pledge abstinence from alcohol, and any other controversial behavior.

The Buildup to Merger

Comparing the size, the structure, and the style of the two youth organizations in 1950 is instructive. According to the Joint Relations Committee, which prepared the merger plan, the two groups measured up as follows just as the merger process began:

	AUY	*UYF*
Membership	2,432	4,000 approx.
Number of groups affiliated	221	246
Age range	14-25 (average, 17)	12-25
Regional distribution	New England 47%	New England & New York 55%
	Mid Atlantic 13%	Mid Atlantic 3%
	Midwest 20%	Midwest 22%
	Other 20%	Other 20%
Organization	Council of 20 with 4 elected officers	Board of 9 with 4 elected officers
	14 regional representatives	4 trustees representing task-oriented departments
	1 past president	
	1 UYF representative	1 AUY representative

The fact that the joint publication of the two groups only had a circulation of 1,600 suggests that the membership figures above might have been high estimates, especially for UYF. They probably included a sizeable number of junior-high youth as well. Although the distribution of members is almost the same in both groups, the AUY's leadership and strength was more evenly distributed across the continent.

Alice Harrison described the American Unitarian Youth as a much more highly politicized organization than the Universalist Youth Fellowship. Its size and election procedures produced a very aggressive style of leadership, which made many UYF state conventions nervous about the merger. Harrison commented, "The Unitarian youth, bless their hearts, could argue the Universalists out of anything."

Richard Woodman remembered the aura of solemnity and importance around the Unitarian headquarters at 25 Beacon Street in the years of Frederick May Eliot. The first time he attended a meeting there, representing UYF on a joint committee, he was very surprised to receive a voucher for his personal expenses in making the trip down to Boston from Maine. The AUY did have more money than UYF, reflecting its greater institutional strength. Universalist congregations and youth groups tended to be rural rather than urban. UYF leaders went to Tufts and to St. Lawrence University, while the Unitarians attended Harvard and Antioch.

On the other hand, the Universalists had a closer and more trusting relationship to their adult denomination than the Unitarians did. The UCA leadership, which was younger than the AUA, had closer ties to the youth. Following merger, the LRY's first office would be located at the Universalist headquarters at 16 Beacon Street rather than in the larger Unitarian building at 25 Beacon.

The UYF's withdrawal from the joint publication of *The Young Liberal* had not indicated any alienation between the two youth groups. On the contrary, interest in merger had never been greater. Merger was in the air in denominational terms as well. The 1947 AUA convention had passed a resolution calling for an exploration of the possibility of merger with the Universalists. In 1949, when a joint AUA-UCA Commission on Union was set up, a merger within the following three years appeared imminent. The final result of this commission's work was the establishment of the Council of Liberal Churches, which was to develop joint publications and publicity for the two denominations to supplement the cooperative religious education program that already existed.

In the summer of 1949, amidst talk of denominational merger, the first steps toward the creation of a joint youth program, Liberal Religious Youth, were taken. At their summer annual meetings, the American Unitarian Youth, with Charles Eddis as president, and the Universalist Youth Fellowship, led by Carl Seaburg, each passed resolutions inviting the other to hold their 1951 conferences and annual meetings together.

Leon Hopper and Charles Collier served as presidents of AUY and UYF, respectively, during the preparatory year of 1950-1951. A Joint Relations Committee, consisting of six Unitarians, six Universalists, and the two staff people (Harrison and Henniges), was charged with planning the 1951 conference. At the 1950 annual meetings, that committee was formally instructed to conduct a thorough exploration of the possibilities and process of a merger of the two youth groups and supervise the conference arrangements. During the interval between these 1949 resolutions and the 1951 joint conference, UYF and AUY published a good deal of joint material experimentally: a Youth Sunday guide, a songbook, *The Youth Leader*, and *The Liberal's Challenge*, as well as material explaining the plans and issues around merger.

The Creation of Liberal Religious Youth

The joint conference of 1951 was held at Camp Idlewild on an island in Lake Winnepesaukee, New Hampshire. The registration fee was eight dollars. Delegates from far away benefited from a travel equalization fee.

The isolation of the camp led to concerns and speculation

about the rules of conduct. Sure enough, a small party was discovered drinking on the back side of the island one night, well after lights-out. The council supervising the conference had the unpleasant responsibility of asking the guilty parties to leave the island.

Both the American Unitarian Association and the Universalist Church of America were represented at Lake Winnepesaukee by their top leadership. Robert Cummins, superintendent of the UCA, and AUA president Frederick Eliot both addressed the convention mid-week. Boat schedules made it necessary for Eliot to spend the night on the island. True to form, one of the skits presented during the AUY's program that evening featured a grand lampoon of the president.

The youth groups printed information about each other and their respective denominations. The week's theme speaker was Tracy Pullman, then minister of the merged Universalist Unitarian Church of Detroit. Each organization met in a separate business session to discuss and vote on the report of the Joint Relations Committee (JRC).

The JRC Report came in the form of a very well-balanced "pro and con" statement. It did not recommend rapid moves toward merger. Although favoring a fully organic union, the committee advocated moving slowly, taking at least three years. The report recommended local and regional interactions as well as executive-level joint decision-making and cooperation. Expressing some concern for continuity, the JRC supported the continuation of an adult professional staff and a youth-adult committee at the denominational level. It suggested that all appointments to these positions be made by a Personnel Committee comprised equally of youth and adults.

The staff situation was of particular concern at this conference, for the AUY Council asked for and received the resignation of Paul Henniges as the AUY director. The convention passed a controversial resolution that read,

> Should at any time the staff situation become unfavorable,
> the youth movement, after consultation with the Youth

Activities Committee, shall have the power to discontinue the professional services of the staff member.

Eventually both groups, in their separate sessions, endorsed a two-year plan for merger, to culminate in 1953 with the Joint Relations Committee and the two executive boards handling the transition. The two presidents chosen to carry through the process were Rozelle Royall, elected by UYF, and Leon Hopper, re-elected by the AUY. The JRC was commissioned to prepare bylaws and program materials to facilitate the merger, and the two groups voted to meet again in joint conventions in 1952 and 1953. Meanwhile, they expanded their joint publications and consultations.

In 1952 the AUY and AUA appointed Sam Wright as executive director of the AUY. The formation of LRY would include making Wright its executive director. While serving in the director's position for three years, throughout the merger period, Wright wrote the words to what became known as "the LRY hymn." It continues to appear (with a few lyric changes) in the hymnal *Singing the Living Tradition* under the title "We Would Be One," using the same tune chosen by Wright, "Finlandia," by Sibelius:

We would be one, as now we join in singing
Our hymn of youth, to pledge ourselves anew
To that high cause of greater understanding
Of who we are, and what in us is true.
We would be one in living for each other
To show mankind a new community.

We would be one, in building for tomorrow
A greater world than we have known today.
We would be one, in searching for the meaning
Which binds our hearts, and points us on our way.
As one we pledge ourselves to greater service
With love and justice strive to make men free.

In 1952, the AUY-UYF joint convention tentatively approved a constitution for the merged organization, in spite of some concern on the Universalist side that the process was happening too fast. The leadership of both organizations worked furiously to meet the merger schedule, setting the stage for the final vote.

At the 1953 AUY-UYF joint convention, held at Hanover College in Hanover, Indiana, the by-laws were reviewed and revised. The final merger votes took place in separate business sessions. Harrison recalls that before the last vote in Hanover, discussion took seven hours, "without eating, without sleeping, without hardly getting up to go to the john,"

The Universalist side still expressed a little reluctance, registering forty-seven "yes" to four "no" votes. Some of the four negative votes had been cast in accordance with instructions from the delegates' local groups or churches. Both sides, however, voted overwhelmingly in favor of merger. In joint session, they made the motion formally unanimous.

Participants experienced some difficulty selecting the name for their new organization. Beyond concerns within each group about losing their denominational identities, the Canadians were reluctant to endorse the title "Liberal Religious" because of possible confusion with Canada's Liberal Party. Yet the name "Liberal Religious Youth" emerged as by far the most popular choice, and Liberal Religious Youth it became.

Over the two years since the joint 1951 conference, the AUY and UYF governing bodies had met together and made decisions in joint sessions as much as possible. Royall had served as UYF president throughout the merger process, with Eileen Layton taking over from Hopper as AUY president from 1952 to 1953.

LRY's first continental convention and its incorporation as a separate successor organization did not take place until 1954. The AUY and UYF boards continued to function in a parallel fashion until then, but for all intents and purposes the newly merged Executive Board structure began functioning after the 1953 conference.

The structure incorporated the basic AUY form, with features of the UYF. The convention elected four officers to staggered two-year terms. Filling out the governing board were seventeen representatives sent by their respective regions. Clara Mayo, having served as the last AUY president from 1953 to 1954, was elected the first president of LRY.

Age limits had to be set for the new LRY. Twenty-five would certainly be the top age limit, but what about the junior-high people? In a compromise move, it was decided that voting members were to be fourteen to twenty-five years old, although local groups could include members as young as twelve.

Following the Hanover convention, a group of new LRY members traveled forty-strong to Andover, Massachusetts, where representatives of the Unitarian and Universalist churches were meeting in joint session in an attempt to found the Council of Liberal Churches. The LRY members gave a presentation on their merger process and contributed greatly to the spirit and work of that gathering.

With the merger, LRY adopted a more cordial relationship with the professional staff and the two denominations. Staff was hired by a Joint Personnel Committee and paid from AUA and UCA money. Sam Wright became the executive director of LRY, while Alice Harrison became associate director for high school programs and Layton became associate director for college activities (i.e., the Channing-Murray Foundation).

The creation of LRY was not only significant to the liberal youth movement, it played a crucial role in the history of Unitarianism and Universalism as a whole, showing the Unitarian and Universalist churches, which had been dancing around the issue of merger for years, that merger could be successfully accomplished, and perhaps more importantly, that it was inevitable.

For the youth, the creation of LRY was the beginning of a new era. As Hopper observed, "With the completion of a successful merger, and augmented by an independent staff (responsible to the LRY Council) the theme of 'youth autonomy' and independence became even stronger."

ᘓ

Around 1950, the First Universalist Church in Norway, Maine, had a vigorous youth program going. Norway was a town of 5,000 people then, some 45 miles in from Portland on the coast and not too near any large city. A few shoe factories were its main industry, and it proudly called itself the Snowshoe Capital of the World. A large lake on the edge of town attracted many summer people. One of the local wits achieved some notoriety for his retort to one of the summer people, who asked him what the townspeople did after the visitors left. "We fumigate," was his terse reply.

The Universalist and Congregational churches were the principal Protestant churches in the community, with small Baptist, Methodist, and Episcopal chapels serving their communicants. The single Roman Catholic church served several surrounding towns. A considerable settlement of Finns had, a generation or so earlier, moved into the area and added a special flavor to the region.

When I came to this town, at the end of World War II, I found an active junior high youth program, with some fifteen youngsters under the capable lay leadership of Mrs. Ruth Russell. Shortly after my arrival, a high school youth program was started, and the group decided to call itself the Norway Universalist Youth (NUY). An active church school, a Cub Scout program, an off-again on-again Boy Scout troop, and occasionally a junior choir of youngsters to supplement the adult senior choir completed the youth program of the church.

From thirty to fifty youngsters took part in the two youth groups, moving almost automatically from one to the other. Each group developed traditions that continued year after year and became events that members looked forward to. Both groups were active participants in the state-wide youth programs of the denomination, with carloads attending all the various youth rallies held in the state. One memorable occasion was the 250-mile trek from Norway to Caribou in the northernmost part of the state for a three-day youth gathering that was happily remembered for many seasons. Three or four of these state rallies would be attended each year. Since Ferry Beach was in Maine, a goodly number of the youth group members attended summer youth programs there and looked forward to the annual Ferry Beach reunion in the spring.

A smaller number attended New England youth meetings, and in August, 1949, the Norway youth groups hosted the sixtieth national convention of the Universalist Youth Fellowship. This involved much planning on the part of the hosts and featured the usual business sessions, workshops, a carnival, a beach outing at the lake, a grand ball, and a street dance when the town blocked off the main street and joined in the festivities with their weekend visitors. More than a hundred young people registered, and a great many others were around for the affair.

The Junior High Fellowship ordinarily met on Sundays at 5:00 pm and once a month had a supper which they prepared themselves, with a little guidance from their advisors, who had to eat the repast too. A lot of physical activity marked their programs. A look at the old folders shows that in any one year the group would go roller skating at the local rink, swimming at the Hebron Academy pool, bowling, folk dancing, dancing at a record party, climbing some of the local "mountains," hiking on Sunday afternoons to interesting local spots, and the like.

They visited other nearby local Universalist youth groups and invited them back to their meetings. Speakers came in on topics that might have some appeal at their level of interests. There might be a debate on the value of comic books (a hot issue then!). The Mormon elders might be invited over, a filmstrip on the United Nations would be shown, and so on. Sometimes they would have a "home talent" night or visit one of the local industries. Always, a short worship service led by one of the members preceded the evening activities.

The NUY meeting, Sundays at 7:00 pm repeated the pattern of many of these programs with some additional items. One of their eagerly anticipated events was the annual winter trip when the whole group (after raising money to pay for it) went off on a long weekend that included skiing, tobogganing, snow shoeing, building snow forts and having snowball fights outside, and much card playing, bull sessions, horsing around, and general good fun inside. One year they camped out in a parishioner's cabin to which the only access was across a frozen lake. Supplies had to be towed in on a toboggan, and drinking water had to be chopped out of the lake. Several years in a row they went up to Gilead to Si and Mary Cole's place. Mary's good cooking and Si's fiddle livened up the time spent there. Coming home the first time we went there, we were treated to a magnificent display of the aurora borealis, the first time many of us had seen this spectacular sky event.

Another annual event was the minstrel show. It was given in traditional blackface the first year, but the minister had a problem with this, which was talked over candidly within the group. The solution for succeeding shows was to present the minstrel show in other guises. Holding to the basic pattern of a minstrel show—with an interlocutor, end men (ah, the sexist days of old!), a chorus, specialties, and a barrelful of corny jokes—they presented in succession a circus minstrel, a Gay Nineties minstrel, a Western minstrel, a Broadway minstrel, and so on. Started by Mrs. Ernestine Brown, advisor of the NUY, the shows were ably assisted by Bess Klain and Vern Whitman as the sparkling pianists. The younger youth group joined the NUY for this annual shindig and looked forward to the time when they could take some of the leading parts. Tickets were only fifty cents (which went a lot further then) and audiences of two hundred or more would come. Often there would be a quarter of that number up on stage singing their lungs out.

Deep intellectual meetings were in short supply, unfortunately, much to the regret of the minister, though some attempts were made in this direction. Fun and fellowship were the strong points, and the social message had to wiggle in the back door. For instance, one night the NUY had a "Chinese Night" with the Junior High Fellowship as their guests. Everyone attending had to take off their shoes at the door. The committee sported kimonos. The worship service included an old Chinese folksong, the reading of Taoist, Confucianist, and Buddhist scriptures, and in conclusion, a hearty rendering of "In Christ There Is No East Or West." The meal was eaten sitting cross-legged on the floor. Subsequently a Finnish evening and a

Pennsylvania Dutch evening were planned. These events took a lot of preparation but were greatly enjoyed.

One useful byproduct of this active participation of the youth in the life of the church was that many of the young men of the high school group, starting with Stanton Anderson, served as janitors to the church and provided splendid custodial care.

Looking back after twenty-five years, it would seem that an active happy social life was provided that reached out and embraced many who had not previously been associated with that Universalist church. A number of them who stayed on in the community are still active in its concerns today.

Carl Seaburg
Norway, Maine

LRY Comes of Age

With the creation of Liberal Religious Youth, the two denominations gave one youth organization the responsibility for all of their high school and college programming. Both the American Unitarian Association and the Universalist Church of America now contributed to LRY's budget. Relating to two separate denominational bureaucracies created more complicated communication between youth and adult leaders than before, but also made the youth organization more functionally independent. A Joint Youth Advisory Committee, composed of Unitarian and Universalist leaders and LRY members, was set up to facilitate communication and cooperation in funding and programming.

The first continental convention of Liberal Religious Youth took place in 1954 at Chesire Academy in Chesire, Connecticut. It was followed by the International Religious Fellowship's annual conference, held in America for the first time since 1936.

Signs of Strain

After the Chesire convention, the youth leadership and conference delegates called the professional staff on the carpet during the annual IRF meeting. In effect they were asking them to justify their jobs and the manner in which they had been performing them.

It had been a hot day and a long meeting, and everyone was a little cranky. Sam Wright and Eileen Layton got up and gave a verbal account of their work above and beyond the written report they had handed in. Then it was Alice Harrison's turn. As she remembers it, she stood up in front of the convention and said quietly, "You have my report. I don't know what else to say, except that never before in my professional career has anyone ever asked me to defend the job I've given my life to. So I have nothing to say." No one else had anything more to say either. The matter was dropped and the meeting moved on to other things. Apparently the air had not been cleared, though, for in the fall of 1954, Sam Wright accepted a call back to the parish ministry and resigned his position as LRY executive director. A Personnel Committee was organized with representation from both denominations. The LRY leadership at this point was still made up primarily of college students. Though a few had undergone two years of military service, interrupting their LRY careers, the top age among these leaders was twenty-one.

In the past, AUY had followed a staffing pattern of seeking out parish ministers who seemed appropriately qualified and attempting to lure them to an attractive Boston-based job with lots of travel opportunities. However, members of the Personnel Committee who met in late 1954 decided they really wanted a person with a lot of experience in developing youth programs, even if that person had to be found outside the denomination. Their eventual choice, Bill Gold, did come from outside the Unitarian Universalist fold. In many ways, his experience and objective insight into LRY's situation was just what the organization needed. However, it would not be long before this hopeful situation began to sour.

Gold began work in early 1955, joining Harrison and Layton on the professional staff. At the continental convention held that year in Olivet, Michigan, Robert Johnson was elected LRY president for the coming year.

On May 27, 1956, after only fifteen months as executive director, Gold resigned to accept a call into the parish ministry. The decision was a blow to the LRY leaders. They blamed themselves for the tensions and the shortcomings in Gold's relationship with them and with LRY as an organization, as reflected in a resolution they passed after formally receiving Gold's resignation:

> Whereas, there has been insufficient communication among the staff members, and
>
> Whereas the personal relations among leaders of LRY have been overstressed, and
>
> Whereas these shortcomings may have hindered the realization of LRY's stated programs,
>
> Be it resolved, that LRY recognize these errors and strive to overcome them.

Certainly the youth leadership had not been able to listen to Gold's concerns, or follow the directions in which he wanted to move. However, his decision to resign involved other factors. Gold came from outside the two denominations into a working situation with an inherited staff (Harrison and Layton) who had a closer relationship with and understanding of LRY. The concept of "youth autonomy" had functioned in LRY as more of an ideological backdrop than a well-defined blueprint for responsibility and decision-making. Gold understood youth autonomy in LRY intellectually, but he could never strike the right balance of power in his relationship to the Executive Committee and the council. Neither side could communicate its positions adequately to the other.

In his relationship with the two denominations, Gold faced the same frustrations every succeeding executive director would encounter. LRY's size and needs were clearly growing, and the financial support offered by the UCA and the AUA was not keeping up. Many of Gold's ideas and goals were out of reach due to lack of funds. At the time of his resignation, the UCA was forced to cut back its support even further, making Harrison's resignation from her job inevitable. She resigned the following year to work within the new junior high program of the Council of Liberal Churches.

Gold accepted the pulpit of the Unitarian church in Schenectady, New York. His letter of resignation, final report, and some "brief observations" that he wrote as the job ended indicate that many problematic themes that would plague LRY for the next two decades were already full-blown in the mid-1950s. A particular concern for Gold was the tension between LRY's role as a "service organization" for the youth of the Unitarian and Universalist denominations and its significance as an experience-centered extended family:

> It has been my conviction that LRY's program must go beyond the experience-centered type of program it has had in the past, important as this emphasis is. I have therefore sought to make my work with LRY as much as possible a work of rendering services to local churches...feeling that otherwise LRY would become an organization offering a limited experience to a limited number of youth leaders.

Some commentators have perceived the changes LRY underwent in the late 1960s the results of a "takeover" of LRY's structure by young people more alienated from and distrustful of the social milieu they grew up in than past LRY members had been. Gold's observations of 1956, however, zero in on problems that would continue to plague LRY throughout the 1960s and 1970s:

> Many of the most devoted young people lack the kind of experience which would make their devotion to LRY truly invaluable. They have never had the experience of being in a strong local group or of participating in a complete and well-organized youth program. To them the liberal religious youth group is a source of security in their eccentricity. This is a valuable contribution the group should make to youth who might otherwise be lonely in their individuality, but if it is the dominant force in the life of the group or the individual, it results in a distorted concept of LRY's program and purposes. Young people with such a background are more likely to be more concerned about maintaining the organization and manipulating the structure than about developing its program and advancing its fundamental purposes.

This is a logical concern, since they lack the knowledge and experience to develop programs, and they are primarily concerned with preserving the structure that has made them feel significant. However, if LRY is to carry the burden of liberal religious education for the entire youth of two great denominations, it must do more than preserve its unique organization.

Gold left the LRY Council with a number of recommendations. They included more leadership training for LRY leaders on the local and regional levels; a separation of the college and high school programs; encouragement of adults to take more sympathetic interest in and to better support LRY's programming, and a budget of at least $35,000-$40,000, providing for three professional staff and two secretaries.

With Harrison's resignation also upon them and finances dismal, the council requested Layton's resignation from the staff in order to begin with a clean slate.

The year 1956-1957 was one of introspection and review for LRY's leadership. LRY established a Committee on Planning and Review, with youth and adult membership, in addition to the Personnel Committee, which was searching for a new executive director. The Joint Youth Activities Committee took an important role in filling the gap that year, as did a special joint committee of the Council of Liberal Churches and LRY, which particularly investigated the relation between LRY high-school and college programs.

Richard Teare was elected LRY president in the 1957 LRY continental convention, which went by with no announcement of the new executive director. That fall, Leon Hopper was appointed to the position.

New Directions

Hopper began work officially in December 1957 although, he had been on hand as a member of the Liberal Religious Youth Advisory Committee for the midwinter council meetings and the 1957 annual conference in Jones Gulch. He was twenty-nine at the time, and only six years away from his own experience as an LRY leader.

Hopper was responsible for services to high school and college youth of two denominations in six hundred churches, with a full-time staff of one director and one secretary and a $27,000 budget. At the winter meetings, his first report to the LRY Council was an indictment of LRY's current predicament, a strong statement that would set the tone for his six years on the job:

> The fact is that LRY *has not produced*—it has not captured the interest and support of our churches which it should have, it has not made a mark on the high school youth, it has barely touched the college student. You have not been able to attract the professional leadership you need—you have not been able to provide the resources demanded, or render the services requested . . . . To be very frank, LRY is entering a period of trial . . . . It is my strong feeling that LRY is in a rut— that the ways in which it has done things in the past will not be adequate to meet the demands of our new responsibilities. LRY is going to have to be willing to use new approaches —to revolutionize itself.

Hopper proposed a four-point policy on program production that established the pattern LRY followed in its printed programs through the 1960s. He recommended that LRY commit to producing a variety of program resource materials for use by local groups, with the major responsibility for development of these materials to rest with the executive director. He asked the council to budget for the editorial development as well as production of these materials, with the end goal that the sale of materials would cover the cost of production. Hopper was dissatisfied with the communication between the continental convention and the council. He made his particular skills and goals clear to the council and asked for a free hand and support in accomplishing those goals. His relationships with the five LRY executive committees and councils he worked with seem to have been mutually satisfying. Leon Hopper provided the kind of continuity and vision that LRY badly needed at that time, and the organization went through a growth spurt during his tenure. That partly reflected growth in the adult denomination, but also represented better organization and communication between Boston and the local and regional groups.

New LRY groups and federations came into being, and more began to affiliate and pay dues. During Hopper's six years leading LRY, the number of active federations grew from twenty-one to thirty-three. Some of the increase resulted from old federations expanding and splitting apart. These developments led to regional committees forming to coordinate activities in geographical areas that had numerous federations. New regional committees sprang up that modeled themselves after the New England Regional Committee (NERC), which had formed within AUY in 1946. The Midwest Regional Committee (MICON) was established in October 1958 at a large meeting in Chicago, soon followed by the Middle Atlantic Regional Committee (MARC) and the Southeast LRY.

LRY, Inc.

Since the merger that formed LRY, the organization had experienced difficulty with its corporate status. It needed a distinct status, apart from the Unitarian and Universalist denominational organizations, because it was funded by both but controlled by neither. Initially, the question of where to incorporate had become an issue because Massachusetts law required corporations registered there to hold their annual meetings in the state. The intention of holding the annual meetings together with the continental convention, at varying sites, made the LRY incorporators decide in 1953 to register the corporation in Delaware, which had no such requirement. However, Massachusetts law did not permit the invested capital of the AUY and the UYF to be transferred to a Delaware corporation.

The LRY Council then petitioned the Massachusetts legislature to make an exception to its corporate laws due to the circumstances of LRY's operations. The legislature accepted the petition, and in 1956, LRY finally incorporated in Massachusetts under a special legislative act.

Over the first few annual meetings, the new LRY Council established a pattern of doing business that would remain stable through the following twelve years. The LRY bylaws specified the basic regional divisions from which the council representatives would be drawn. These regional groups would divide and subdivide into separate federations as LRY grew, but the voting distribution set up by the early council remained stable.

The council structured its meetings so that topic-oriented commissions did most of the ground work in their respective areas during the week of council meetings. At the end of the week, each commission would come back with specific recommendations for the whole council to consider and vote on. This structure was maintained from 1954 through the LRY board meetings of 1968.

Expanding International Involvement

During the 1950s, contact with the IRF had been maintained mainly through the efforts of Eileen Layton. As the AUY's official delegate to the 1951 IRF conference in Switzerland, Layton had begun an association with IRF which lasted until she left LRY's employ in 1957. When she returned to Europe in 1952 under AUY's sponsorship, she had been elected second vice president of IRF. Her efforts had brought the 1954 conference to America, where she had organized a three-month program of touring and study for the eleven Europeans who came over for the conference in Chesire.

Two major issues marked that period in IRF's history. The first went directly to the heart of IRF's understanding of itself and its purposes.

After World War II, the free religious congregations of Germany had reorganized themselves and re-established their international contacts. The first post-war IRF gathering in England had extended a special resolution of support and good will to

German youth, but no meaningful contact had been made until 1950. As the new youth groups in these churches developed, they identified with the more humanist orientation of the free religious churches with which they were affiliated.

Ruth Neuendorffer of America made the first official contact with the German groups, and IRF president Ronald McGraw of England was instrumental in arranging a tour of England for the Offenbach Free Religious Youth in 1951. Later in the summer of 1951, the Germans applied for membership in the IRF as a united group, calling themselves "Freireligiouse Jugenbund Deutschlands" (The Free Religious Youth Group of Germany, or FJD).

The strongest member groups of the IRF at that time were the Swiss "Zwinglibund" and Dutch representatives. Both groups were affiliated with the Free Christian, or Free Protestant, churches in their countries, which maintained their identity as Christians. They were unwilling to consider admitting non-Christian groups to the IRF. When the issue came to the floor of the business meeting in 1951, it was tabled with no consensus reached.

Layton brought a report of the meeting back to the 1951-1952 AUY Council meetings over Christmas, 1951. The Council strongly favored expanding IRF from an exclusively Christian group to include all other "liberal religious group" and had indicated this in resolutions at previous meetings and at the conventions of 1950 and 1951 (it would affirm this position again in 1952). Finally in 1953, the FJD was voted in as a member group of IRF, after a year of written communication about the matter. That move was important in opening up the IRF to include the broader definition of "liberal religion" that prevailed in American Unitarianism and Universalism.

Another project that IRF members became deeply involved in at that time was the founding of Albert Schweitzer College in Switzerland. In 1949, Professor Hans Casparis of Chur, Switzerland, himself an old IRF member, began a summer study camp which he called Modern International College (MIC). He wanted to build MIC into a fully accredited year-round college, providing a broader undergraduate liberal education than was then available in larger established schools. IRF gave moral and financial support to the idea, with member groups adopting a fundraising quota for the college.

The Americans favored a 1952 attempt to merge the Secretariat of the IRF with Modern International College and make it a permanent Secretariat in Switzerland. That plan was never realized. MIC finally acquired its own building. On May 5, 1953, the college purchased a thirty-room hotel in Churwalden, Switzerland, for about $10,000. Having established a home and a program, Professor Casparis approached Dr. Albert Schweitzer for permission to name the college after him. Schweitzer was delighted to give his blessing, so in the fall of 1953, Albert Schweitzer College opened its doors with twenty-five students from five countries.

The college program concentrated on small classes, with informal but intensive study groups under the tutelage of a professor-advisor. The undergraduate program was a two-year interdisciplinary study of Western civilization. Many IRF and LRY members would become involved in Albert Schweitzer College over the course of its existence. At its first summer study session in 1953, some twenty-three Americans attended, including Layton and Wright.

The summer of 1958 marked a turning point in LRY international involvement. Only eleven Europeans had come to America for the first LRY-IRF joint conference in 1954. However, through Layton's efforts, a full contingent of thirty LRY members went to Europe the following summer to participate in the 1955 IRF conference in Barnston, England. Layton functioned that year as IRF advisor and operated the IRF Secretariat out of Boston.

The IRF, in accordance with an American goal, was gradually achieving a more democratic structure. During Layton's IRF involvement, a Nominating Committee was elected for the first time, and the commissions at conferences were expanded so that all delegates could participate. The IRF Executive Committee began to meet at mid-year in addition to its annual meeting in conjunction with the conference.

A big buildup and careful planning within LRY preceded the 1958 American IRF conference, held in Madison, Wisconsin, in conjunction with the Sixteenth Congress of the International Association for Religious Freedom. LRY organized a thirty-day tour of the United States and Canada in private automobiles for the twenty-seven European guests.

The tour ended at the IARF Congress, which was followed by the IRF conference, based on the theme "Social Welfare: Who Cares?" After the conference—attended by seventy-six delegates from seven countries—many participants migrated to Guilford College in Guilford, North Carolina, for the 1958 LRY convention. There, Spencer Lavan, who had coordinated arrangements for the Madison IRF conference, was elected LRY president.

The admission of the German group, Freireligiose Jugendbund Deutschelands, and the general liberalizing tendency within IRF continued to produce changes within its membership. The Dutch group (VCJC) was becoming less and less committed to IRF, paying minimal membership dues by the early 1960s, but a group called "Dutch Friends of IRF" was taking a more active role at conferences. The humanist element in the FJD finally split off from the rest of the organization and began to associate with the youth organization of the International Humanist and Ethical Union, made up mostly of groups in northern Germany. Those in the area of Frankfurt, Mainz, and Offenbach continued their IRF affiliation, and in the late 1950s a new group in the south of Germany, "Freichristliche Jugendbund" (FCJ), came into IRF.

Albert Schweitzer College continued its program but without the close ties to IRF that it had maintained at its inception.

The Channing-Murray Program

After the flurry of activity in programming for college-age people during the late 1940s, such programs had again fallen into neglect at the denominational level. In the year 1947-1948, the Channing Foundation of the AUY had some eighty-eight groups registered.

By 1953, when LRY was born, the number had dropped to fifteen. The Universalists had even fewer groups and only kept in touch with them by mail.

The most consistent programming for college students continued to come out of the churches themselves on a regional and local basis. The Western Unitarian Conference set up its own College Centers Committee (CCC) in 1951, and the Channing Foundation cooperated with existing regional college programs sponsored by the Metropolitan Area Council in New York State, in Maine, and in the Boston area.

When LRY was created, Eileen Layton took on specific responsibility for the new Channing-Murray program. *The Liberal's Challenge* continued as a regular college-age periodical under her supervision. By 1955, after two years of organizing, the number of existing Channing-Murray groups had climbed back to about eighty-nine. This represented the peak of the program; groups declined after Layton left the LRY staff in 1957.

Urbana, Illinois, enjoyed what was by far the most successful campus-based program within Channing-Murray. Arnold Westwood, the minister in the Urbana Church and a former AUY president, had co-founded the program with Earl McKinney. During the 1950s, its budget, based on area church contributions and grants from the AUA, averaged around $1,250 a year, supporting a staff of three, with one working full-time. The program involved topic-oriented seminars among members, well-known guest speakers on campus and at the church, social events, and a regular coffee house called The Red Herring. Such local programs flourished on their own with the help of interested ministers and a good core of student leaders, but in the early 1950s, only New England, Ohio, and Illinois developed regional activity of any kind.

As early as the late 1940s, talk of separating the college-age programming from the increasingly high school-oriented LRY had begun. In her 1953 Channing-Murray report, Layton commented, "AUY is sadly deficient in its college approach; is AUY really two organizations, high school and college, in one, and if it is, shouldn't we recognize it as such?" Although the AUA began to take a more direct hand in promoting college work in the late 1950s, this whole area continued to be a point of tension with LRY.

A motion passed at the 1957 LRY continental convention addressed this tension by creating two councils within LRY. One served high-school youth and the other served college-age youth, with biennial continental conventions and separate leadership training conferences in the interim. The plan would eventually prove ineffective and be superceded by other ideas. However, it created distinct programming vehicles for the two groups within the structure of the continental convention.

The AUA College Centers Committee, dating from the 1940s, cooperated with the AUY and LRY programs but met with the same limited success. Yet sociological analyses of the membership of AUA would invariably conclude that the colleges were gold mines of potential members; that the college years are a time for seeking one's religious identity and questioning the religious environment that one has been raised in; and that the AUA was missing the boat in its approach to college programming. In 1956, an opportunity arose to test these theories. The General Alliance of Unitarian Women had raised a special Diamond Jubilee Fund of $18,000 which they wished to donate to the American Unitarian Association. At the suggestion of Frederick Eliot, it was earmarked for college work, allowing a revival of the College Centers Committee. Reconstituted as a foundation, the CCC made grants to local college centers' programs and administered the Billings Fund, which sponsored lectures on college campuses. The lectures were particularly directed at colleges with a strong Unitarian presence.

The Unitarian CCC operated independently of the Channing-Murray Foundation, which was Unitarian and Universalist. However, a further influx of funds into college programming would bring the two programs closer together. Following the sudden death of Frederick May Eliot (February 17, 1958), Dana McLean Greeley was elected on May 1, 1958, to fill the remaining three years of Eliot's term as president of the AUA. Greeley launched a capital campaign entitled The Development Fund. Its goal was primarily to raise money for programs rather than endowment capital. The Development Fund pledged $250,000 toward college work over a period of years.

Nothing like that sum was ever spent, but the proposal produced early results. Leon Hopper was able to get the extra staff member he had been wanting. In 1959, Orloff Miller was hired as associate director of LRY, with a major responsibility in college work. Miller was to work closely with the CCC, serve as its secretary, and become the only staff person in touch with all three prongs of Unitarian college programming (the national College Centers, Channing-Murray, and local and regional College Centers).

A major problem with the College Centers approach had to do with evaluation. With grants given left and right, local programs began and flourished, but it was very difficult to determine the degree to which these programs influenced the students' view of liberal religion. The primary motive behind these programs as far as the AUA was concerned was extension, based on the thesis that colleges were ripe orchards of new members. The period from 1958 to 1969 represents the most successful approach to college programming in the history of the youth movement, but no studies have been done on the lasting effect it had on the individuals involved or on the Unitarian Universalist movement as a whole.

The Unitarian-Universalist Merger

For its first six years of existence, LRY had been like the child of separated parents. Both parents supported Junior and both had ideas about how Junior should spend the money. The situation was awkward, but further fostered the autonomy of LRY. By 1959, the momentum toward merging the two denominations was at its peak. The machinery had finally been set in motion to bring the whole issue to some resolution. LRY leaders felt some anxiety about their organization's future in a new, merged denomination. During that period, LRY had been making good use of its Committee on Planning and

Review. Like a Commission of Appraisal within LRY, this committee solicited opinions on the organization's work from an adult advisory group of old AUY, UYF, and LRY members. The participants regularly received a set of questions regarding LRY, and everyone's written responses would be compiled, summarized, and distributed.

In 1958 and 1959, the committee went through a process of evaluating the successes and failures of the LRY merger, while looking ahead to the inevitable merger of the two adult denominations and what consequences that might have for LRY.

Hopper saw the occasion as a time of testing for LRY. He identified many issues that could be addressed as the old structures were re-examined in the light of merger. A major issue involved the old tension of being fundamentally a high-school organization run by college students. Another was the excessive amount of staff time lost in simple maintenance of the institution of LRY. It sapped energy from programming work. These issues were raised and discussed at the 1959 continental convention at Grinnell College in Grinnell, Iowa.

Hopper had clear ideas about the kind of relationship with the denomination that would best deal with these problems and put LRY into a more advantageous position for denominational funding and interest. He recommended, first, a much closer relationship with the denomination on all levels. In particular, he suggested incorporating the LRY professional staff members into the Department of Education of the new denomination, where they would have more status, job security, and stability. Secondly, he suggested separating the high school and college-age programs. Thirdly, he recommended overhauling the old council structure, since it duplicated and paralleled tasks that could be done by the new regional committee organizations.

In 1961, the American Unitarian Association and the Universalist Church of America voted to merge into the Unitarian Universalist Association. Hopper's recommendations for structuring the new UUA-LRY relationships were substantially accepted by all concerned. The LRY executive director became part of the staff of the new Division of Education, paid out of its budget, and a new LRY Advisory Committee was established.

A continental Board of Trustees replaced the LRY Council. The Council had been composed of twenty representatives from "regional groupings" that no longer reflected LRY's federation structure. The new board would be composed of the presidents or representatives of each dues-paying federation. The Executive Committee was realigned to include three directors in addition to its four officers. This new board controlled the funds LRY received from dues and investment income, while the rest of LRY's money came through the Division of Education budget to be used for salaries, office expenses, and staff travel. The total LRY budget amounted to between $23,000 and $25,000.

The LRY annual convention was replaced by the "continental conference," reflecting a new emphasis on program-oriented, rather than business-oriented, conferences.

In a final major change accompanying the denominational merger, LRY voted to become an organization for high-school students. Its bylaws, rewritten to accommodate the new board structure, included an age limit of fourteen to nineteen. A person could be elected to the Executive Committee up to his or her sophomore year in college, but not beyond.

The Creation of SRL

The final separation of the high school program from the college program within LRY arose out of the nearly fifteen years of frustration on the part of college-age people. LRY had been substantially a high school organization from its inception in 1954, but it wasn't until the 1961 Unitarian-Universalist merger that resources became available to form a separate college program.

An Office of College Centers was created within the new UUA structure, to amalgamate the functions of the College Centers Committee and the Channing-Murray program. By 1961, the LRY budget had been allocating some $14,000 to Channing-Murray.

The new College Centers Office appropriated $11,500 of that for its new, separate budget.

Many older LRY leaders, such as Jerry Lewis, Mary Van Wilkins, and Gregg Wood, were interested in working toward a college students' group, but the question remained as to what kind of group it would be. A plebiscite of college-age people within LRY was held to see if there was any support for a group's formation.

At a separate college conference in September 1961 in the Midwest region—the first continental college conference since the resurgence of college-age activity in 1947—the organization Student Religious Liberals (SRL) was formed. Gregg Wood was elected as its first chairman.

SRL began as a small organization. By 1963, it was in touch with just over one-third of the seventeen regional College Centers Committees, which together served over a hundred campus groups. The organization functioned independently of, but in relationship with, Orloff Miller and his office.

SRL's major programs for campus groups in the 1960s consisted of a regular SRL newsletter, "To: SRL," which was sent out to all member groups in cooperation with the Office of College Centers and the annual continental conference. In addition, SRL sponsored *The Liberal Context* and the European Study Tours in co-operation with the Office of College Centers.

The Liberal Context actually pre-dated SRL. In 1960, the College Centers Committee had approached LRY's Channing-Murray Committee concerning a possible joint publishing venture. The result was a high-quality, glossy magazine of scholarly articles, journalism, poetry, and reviews. Its first editor, Dave Cudhea, had been one of the writers and editors responsible for UYF's quality publications in the 1940s. In its magazine format, *The Liberal Context* was the best publication ever associated with the Unitarian Universalist youth movement. The depth and diversity of its content frequently rivaled that of the UUA's *Register-Leader*.

SRL also assumed major responsibility for international contacts, since IRF's membership was largely older than high school age. In 1962, the IRF held its conference jointly with SRL in Springfield, Massachusetts. Another extensive automobile tour was coordinated by David Gilmartin and Spencer Lavan, with forty IRF members participating.

The following year, SRL decided to organize the American trip to Europe for the Dutch IRF conference. This led to annual summer study tours for the next four years. One tour's itinerary included the Soviet Union. At the beginning, SRL and LRY questioned whether high school students should be eligible. Eventually, graduating high school seniors were allowed to participate. Students had to apply for the tours, which had become popular.

Right from the beginning of SRL, an internal contradiction between its goals and its self-definition was apparent. A 1964 statement on the "Concerns and Objectives" of SRL reads in part,

> The most basic personal problem faced by this organization is the coordination of an ultimately personal search with a program of continental and local group organization. How can we serve the personal concerns of liberal religious students without perverting those concerns through the institutional process?

This perceived contradiction would eventually wear SRL down to institutional irrelevance.

Leon Hopper Leaves

Maria Fleming served as LRY president from 1962 to 1963, its first full year of operation under the new bylaws as a completely high school–oriented organization. The year proved disappointing in many ways for Leon Hopper.

Hopper had high hopes for the new relationship between LRY and the UUA. Particularly, he hoped that the closer structural relationship with the UUA, the growth of LRY, and the new sense of denominational involvement among youth would promote greater financial support for youth programs.

However, it soon became apparent that, although new programs were being started with Development Fund money, LRY was not on the priority list for any increases. So Hopper began to look for a ministerial position and submitted his resignation to the LRY board effective August 31, 1963, after he was called to the pulpit in Golden, Colorado.

In his final report to the LRY board, Hopper expressed a certain ambivalence about the concept of "youth autonomy" in LRY and how it should be practiced. He wanted to reduce the suspicion that had become endemic in youth-adult relations, and as he left office, he was beginning to see leadership training programs for both youth and adults as an important step in that direction. (One of the last programs Hopper led was an LRY advisors' workshop in Chicago in May, 1963.)

Hopper also emphasized the importance of field work. He expressed hope for more depth in conference programs, moving beyond mere socializing. His disappointment at the lack of support from the UUA in the face of a very vital program was apparent.

Six years was the longest period of time anyone had stayed on as staff for LRY. The 1950s and early 1960s represented relative stability compared to the upheaval that would rock LRY in the next ten years.

∿

For me, LRY was as much a political awakening as a source for religious inspiration. 1953 was a turning point for me as I completed the spring of my sophomore year at a conservative Episcopal prep school in New York. My family attended All Souls Unitarian church, near our home, where I had been active since second grade. All Souls was then one of the most Christian and conservative of our churches. Its membership was largely conservative in politics as well.

I had always been a gadfly. The previous year I had been the only student in my class at school to show interest in Adlai Stevenson, months before his surprise nomination for the presidency. My belief

in his idealism, his desire to defuse the cold war, his sharp articula-
tion of what America should be—all motivated my being, setting me
apart from my parents and most of my peers, not to mention my
church. The Eisenhower-Nixon mentality had seized most people
around me, and I saw them as people who wanted to hold onto the
world as they saw it.

It is hard to remember exactly when we started a youth group at
the church, but I do remember it survived largely because of the effective leadership of Susannah Wilder (Heinz), a new religious education director. Unlike youth groups in homogeneous suburban or
rural towns, we were a disparate lot, coming from schools all over the
city and having little in common other than that our families attended the church.

While we were in part a "confirmation class" who joined the
church in a memorable formal ceremony in the spring of 1954, we
were also a social group and held short worship services at the close of
our meetings. Seeing that we could not survive on individual Sunday
meetings alone, Sue Wilder took some of us out where there were other
youth, some of whom had convictions similar to my own. This was the
first time I really got to know another minister in a personal way. In
this case it was Vincent Silliman, our great hymnologist, who touched
another important nerve in my being—my love for church music.

But a few months later, an even more important event took
place. At a conference in Montclair, New Jersey, my first overnight
LRY meeting, Donald Harrington of Community Church delivered a
vigorous address on the need to cease nuclear testing. I had never
heard such an outspoken position taken on an issue that concerned
me so deeply. I probably thought him too radical, if anything, and it
would be four years before I discovered some of the far more radical
views of our California religious liberals.

The effect of these two conferences began to overshadow the significance of the local youth group for me as I moved toward gradua-
tion in 1955. At last I had found a greater community, one outside
home and school, with which I could identify. I didn't need to go to
extremes in making my shift. LRY accepted me as I was, and I grew
greatly in LRY. In the summer of 1954, I attended the first merged

continental LRY convention in Connecticut and every convention after that, as well as the 1955 and 1956 IRF European tours, until I completed my term as continental president in 1959.

Spencer Lavan
New York, New York

Cold Buffalo (NY)—
A difficult place for weathering
Hot desires or honest intellect.
But Channing Club
(Sometimes derived from the verb
"to chan" – a pun on changing,
chanting, being serious and close
and honest, & denouncing all
adult hypocrisy)
was a magic circle
full of light, and love,
and the aches of hearts
that grew like weeds –
a fountain
where nourishment was possible
in the midst of the desert.

We ran the show ourselves
(even at that time, that was the most
important thing)
and spoke our righteous indignation
to everyone (especially
Paul Carnes, preaching at him
from his own pulpit).
Our adult advisors practiced
the toleration they preached
(for the most part),
much to our continuing surprise
and loving consternation.

"The Fed" and conferences
punctuated our seasons of hot growth
with international friendships
(some still vital, growing, and among the best
of adult efforts to be ourselves in company)
and all that good talk
(impossible to get
with even your closest friends at school
because of their obedience
to what their parents said was God).
And we ran the show ourselves.
Even at the time, that was the most
important thing.

"Continental" was a mythic story
until I went myself and lived the tribal gatherings
from around the world,
(IARF always sent older kids –
Young men and women who were not as
articulately pioneering,
but sharing in our nervous passions nonetheless).
Turning it into myth while it was happening
with the intensity of our sharing.
And we ran the show ourselves.
Even at the time, that was the most
important thing.

SRL was fun. (We were legal
adults now, so of course we ran the show ourselves.)
But we worked so hard,
and there were so few of us,
we began to get tired of each other's stories
of how damned hard it was
to put an end to that damned war.
("The Denomination" only sold us out in little ways
and our hearts were never truly broken.)

New generations have new dramas
(endless variations on the ancient archetypes
of struggle with the mysteries of being human).
The LRYers I meet now
are confused about the horrors
we adults continue to practice on the world,
upon each other and ourselves,
but on the whole they are more polite
in their refusal to believe our words
are more important than what we are,
than I remember being.

In the on-the-job training
for adult hassles of world stewardship
and adult joys of self-expression,
the best we can do for younger folks (and for ourselves)
is offer money and good counsel,
no strings attached between the two,
remembering the deepest values
of our own experience.

Jeremy Taylor
Buffalo, New York

YPCU convention at Unity Church in Boston (1895)

Automobile sightseeing trip at YPCU convention in Minneapolis/St. Paul (1909). Photo by Hazel Kirk.

YPRU at Star Island (1930)

Oklahoma delegation to AUY conference in Toronto (1949)

AUY/UYF conference in Lake Winnepesake, New Hampshire (1951)

New England-New York UYF rally (1952). Photo by John A. Bachman.

AUY dance (1953)

Joint IRF-SRL conference in Springfield, Massachusetts (1962)

LRY Continental Conference in Santa, Fe, New Mexico (1968)

LRY members march for peace (1970s)

David Knight, member of the LRY Executive Committee, on the way to a Continental Conference (1974 or 1975)

Dedication of Common Ground II at Bowdoin College in Brunswick, Maine (1982)

Gene Pickett and Wayne Arnason at
General Assembly (1982)

YRUU leaders march for jobs, peace, and freedom, Washington, D.C.
(1983)

Spirit circle at Con-Con (1984)

Youth Caucus on plenary floor at General Assembly in Fort Worth, Texas (1994)

The Youth Agenda

PETER BALDWIN entered the world of LRY abruptly in 1963. He had been a minister serving as a chaplain to UU students and faculty at the Massachusetts Institute of Technology when Leon Hopper resigned as executive director of LRY. Baldwin, a former federation advisor in New England, was available to serve as an interim executive director during the search for a permanent replacement. His first continental conference was supposed to be a low-key affair where he could test the waters. However, Hopper came down with appendicitis that week and Baldwin found himself an instant executive director in the midst of what he described as "an exceedingly efficient super-organization."

LRY Leading the Way

It is convenient to think about LRY history before 1969 in the blocks of time marked off by executive directors' terms of office. However, that convenience devalues the importance of the LRY leadership during both Hopper's and Baldwin's tenure. Both had a series of competent, disciplined, and enthusiastic executive committees and boards to work with. A longer history could readily focus on each.

The quality of the youth leadership was particularly strong and important in the transition years after the UU merger, with

Hopper's resignation and Baldwin's arrival on the job. LRY had just become a high school-age organization, and there was a great deal of excitement about that. There was an equal amount of fear about the degree of control that the adult church would try to exert on LRY through the Division of Education.

The LRY executive committees of the early 1960s showed a clear perspective on what LRY was and could be. They understood and practiced an institutional discipline that firmly established LRY's own unique space within the denominational structure. "Youth autonomy" was not merely a theoretical slogan during that time. It was practiced responsibly and thoroughly.

Perhaps part of the reason for the impressive quality of that group of early 1960s executive committees was that they were to some extent an oligarchy. Youth were groomed early for LRY leadership, often moving onto the board and into the Executive Committee predictably, with the vice-president or perhaps one of the directors becoming the next president. Such individuals were usually college sophomores entering their final year in LRY. They had been around a long time and were logical choices. This succession also assured continuity, for a person would routinely have served at least one year on the continental Executive Committee before becoming president.

LRY president Maria Fleming performed a key leadership role in the post-merger organization. Her firm style of chairing board meetings was important for getting the new high school-age board and Executive Committee into top gear.

Chuck Forrester, president from 1963 to 1964, supported the concept of "youth autonomy" articulated by Fleming and strongly believed that to make freedom meaningful, LRY's continental office had to produce top-notch programs for the local groups. The local group was the center of LRY, and federation, regional, and continental activities should serve and relate directly to local situations.

The first result of this commitment to locally directed programs was the LRY Program Packet, field-tested and published in the spring of 1964. Peter Baldwin worked through 1963 and 1964 on the creation of a group assessment guide designed to help a local group evaluate and reach its potential. Fritz West, a director on that year's committee, began work on a creative worship pamphlet that was published during West's term as LRY's next president (succeeding Forrester).

Also in the year 1963-1964, a new LRY magazine was launched through the efforts of Blair Dean, another director on Forrester's committee. Until that time, LRY's primary publication had been *The Youth Leader*, which was begun in 1948 as the UYF periodical. At different stages, it had been published in newspaper and church newsletter formats, combining continental, regional, and local LRY news with advertisements for conferences and products. Dean replaced it with *The Promethean*, an ambitious literary journal in a magazine format. *The Promethean* stands out as LRY's best publishing effort artistically. The magazine minimized local group news, focusing on creative writing, graphics, and thoughtful pieces about UUA/LRY institutional issues.

Capping this burst of publication was Baldwin's "Ministry to Youth," the first of three insightful essays Baldwin wrote about the role of LRY within the UU movement. It had been an exciting and productive year.

Following Baldwin's interim appointment, the Executive Committee, impressed with his style and competence, recommended hiring him on a permanent basis.

From 1964 to 1966, the continental office continued the high standards of local programming set by earlier committees. Monthly local group program and information packets were sent out, new program booklets were developed, and Baldwin's final two "Ministry to Youth" essays appeared.

LRY leaders were looking for more "service projects." The political climate was heating up, youth culture was becoming a more self-conscious entity, and LRY's role within the Unitarian Universalist denomination was under examination. Fritz West, LRY President from 1964 to 1965, expanded the ideology of youth autonomy into a critique of the new denomination. His final report called for LRY to see itself as a "vanguard" in the liberal movement:

> Although our heritage and our fundamental values derive from the Unitarian Universalist ethos, the adults and the youth have formed from that heritage different ideologies and religious perspectives. I have found that LRYers across the continent are uncomfortable with much that the denomination represents; its rationalism, its lack of symbolism, its relevance to the lives of LRYers. By the mere fact of our dissatisfaction, we have a role to play. The role of a catalyst, an agitator, and perhaps, even a vanguard. Too often LRYers view the denomination with disdain, rejecting it as having no meaning and searching elsewhere for the warmth and worth they found in LRY. What these people fail to see is that the ingredients for such an experience and such a religion can be found nowhere else but in the Unitarian Universalist Association. LRY has a religious approach to offer our denomination. Its non-rational religious approach, its modes of creative worship and its perceptions of the religious importance of social action are all a part of the challenge.

The thoughts and feelings represented in this statement would crystallize in diverse programs, political initiatives, and dreams over the next five years. The title for the 1966 continental conference set the tone and the stage: "A Radical Look at Liberal Religion."

Between 1964 and 1965, many of the cultural trends and spiritual innovations that would influence the development of a unique youth culture in the late 1960s and early 1970s were in place. The "human potential movement" was developing in small experiments all over the country, and LRY was one of its testing grounds. Baldwin, working with the Boston University Human Relations Center, developed designs for structured intergenerational encounters and began training and engaging professional group workers to staff LRY conferences. Leadership training conferences held at summer camps used various interpersonal training (T-group) techniques, "marathons," and encounter groups to great effectiveness.

Rumors came from the West Coast of a growing drug scene among young white people. Members of LRY were becoming more open about their sexuality and more adamant in acting out the differences they perceived between their culture and the world of adults. "Sex, drugs and rock' n' roll," which would provoke such widespread cultural anxiety later in the 1960s did not become sources of conflict within LRY until the major media began to notice them in the larger culture. LRY was ahead of the curve, however, in the sense that a UU youth group was one place in the suburbs where white middle- and upper-class youth could encounter cultural innovators, either among their peers or introduced by culturally creative advisors.

By 1965, public conversation about teenage sexual values and behavior had become widespread enough for Bill Sinkford, LRY president from 1965 to 1966, to put together a survey research instrument for use in local groups. Dubbed the "Sinkford Sex Survey," its goal was to gather information on where LRY members' sexual attitudes and values were moving. Besides providing data for LRY's continental leadership, it proved to be a great icebreaker for local group programming around sexuality. (Sinkford, a Harvard college student from Cincinatti, was the first and only African American ever elected president of LRY. In 2001, he became the first African American to be elected president of the UUA.)

The mood of LRY in 1966, when Peter Baldwin was offered a faculty position at Crane Theological School, was confident and strong. In his final report to LRY, Baldwin recommended an ambitious ten-year fundraising program for the support of four new professional LRY field workers. The LRY board accepted a toned-down version of the plan, entitling it "Vanguard in Progress" (VIP). The problems involved in an impending UUA financial and membership decline had not yet become apparent. The Vietnam war was starting to heat up, but at that time, large-scale draft resistance remained a year away. To use Baldwin's phrase, 1966 was the year "before the lid blew off the culture."

Movement Politics in SRL

The Unitarian Universalist youth movement's involvement in the politics of the 1960s is easier to see within SRL's concerns than in the LRY program. LRY printed social responsibility materials and packets for local groups, of course, and political involvement was one subject of the regular litany of exhortation that LRY members heard coming out of the continental office. However, prior to 1967, LRY didn't have a director on its Executive Committee whose primary assignment was social responsibility. SRL members, who were older and located on college campuses, found themselves in the middle of the civil rights movement and involved in the beginnings of the anti-war movement.

In its report on the inauguration of the UUA Department of Social Responsibility, the SRL newsletter quoted a message from Homer Jack, director of that office: "I look forward to working closely with SRL members and groups across the continent. Our Freedom Fund has bailed out several SRL members . . . ."

SRL members numbered among those who answered the call to become civil rights workers in the South during the voter registration campaigns. In the spring of 1965, the entire Unitarian Universalist movement had been mobilized and then shocked by events during the march in Selma, Alabama. A UU minister, James Reeb, was beaten to death on the street in Selma. His companions at the time were Orloff Miller, director of the UUA College Centers Office, and Rev. Clark Olson of Berkeley, California. Their accounts of the slaying would fill the pages of *The Liberal Context*. This event and the beginning of the Free Speech Movement on the Berkeley campus greatly politicized many SRL groups. They organized "free speech movements" on their own campuses, which received coverage in the SRL newsletter and *The Liberal Context*.

The SRL board passed a resolution condemning the war in Vietnam in November 1965 and entered into a program of cooperation with the Students for a Democratic Society. On many campuses, SDS was not allowed to organize, but an SRL group *could* exist, so SDS was able to function behind the skirts of SRL.

In the year 1967-1968, Michael Ferber, who had served as SRL's social responsibility chairman throughout much of this period, was indicted with Dr. Benjamin Spock and others, for conspiracy to resist the draft. The indictment resulted from a service at the Arlington Street Church in which draft cards were burned. Draft resistance, a major political focus for SRL, continued to be an overriding concern after Ferber's trial and acquittal.

The LRY of the 1960s

It's worthwhile to examine whether the LRY scene in the 1960s was really much different from that of the LRY and AUY-UYF groups preceding it in order to understand better why events after Baldwin's departure moved as they did. So many of the most significant characteristics of our youth movement have appeared in recurring patterns over the years: the intensity of interpersonal relationships, the ambivalent relationship with the denomination, the gap between the continental experience and local group realities, the radical critique of the quality of religious community within our churches, and the role of Unitarian and Universalist youth movements as a laboratory for young people to experiment with identity.

Were the LRY board meetings of the 1960s any more creative, disorganized, or fruitful than the first LRY Council meetings of the early 1950s had been? Was there more personal and institutional furor around the youth agenda of 1969 than there had been around the World Federation of Democratic Youth issue in 1948? Was the sexual expression of LRY members of the 1960s any less of an issue than it had been in the 1940s?

Probably not. The dynamics of these situations form analogous patterns. However, some differences about the LRY of the 1960s, many of them well documented in broader analyses of that period, are important to note here.

Between 1960 and 1970, most baby boomers made their turbulent passage through adolescence. The sheer numbers of high school students that LRY was serving or had the potential to serve made their actions very noticeable. They were a self-conscious group of young people, even before the media began to pay so much attention to them in the later part of the decade. Some of this self-consciousness may have been due to the fact that they were being defined for the first time in the late 1950s and early 1960s as a market. The marketing media created a whole world of places and things just for them. However, the media was responding to a developing youth culture as much as it was creating it.

The significance of LRY becoming a high school organization in 1961 cannot be underestimated. Even though the age of leadership had come down to the nineteen- to twenty-one year range already, this organizational change made a difference in the way LRY members viewed themselves and the way the denomination related to them.

From a broader sociological point of view, LRY was an organization in the right place at the right time, insofar as the cultural changes of the mid-1960s were concerned. LRY represented a unique institution within the high-school-aged community. On many parts of the continent, LRY was the only peer-group institution outside the all-pervasive social reality of high school that was neither organizationally nor psychologically dominated by adults. The communications network that LRY represented, with its regional and continental conferences, led people out of their high school and home-town cocoons at an earlier age. So when "the lid blew off the culture," LRY was one of the pressure points where the steam first began to burst through.

Staff Changes

Peter Baldwin's departure in 1966 was a blow to LRY. With younger leadership and less continuity on the Executive Committee, Baldwin's role as a permanent administrator as well as a counselor and group leader were sorely missed. The LRY board of 1966 voted him in as a life member as a token of appreciation.

Ruth Wahtera's Executive Committee of 1966-1967 held the fort during the first half of that year while the Personnel Committee sought a new executive director. The committee's job was considerable, for local and federation activity had reached a real peak. Most of the Wahtera committee was in college. Only a few actually lived in Boston. High-quality local group packets continued to come out monthly.

Early in 1967, Richard Earl Kossow was appointed to the job. Instead of a minister or an old LRY member, the Personnel Committee had selected a UU lay person, a federation advisor from Minnesota whose profession was law. Kossow was a strong personality in the Boston office, but he also placed tremendous faith in the chaotic process of the LRY leadership experience. He supported the directions the LRY members in the office wanted to take. His skills and interests centered more in the field, in the conference situation, than in the administrative area. This was also true of many of the LRY leaders with whom Kossow worked, creating a vacuum in administration.

SRL also went through some staff changes at this time. Orloff Miller resigned from the Office of College Centers in 1966 to return to the parish ministry. His successor, Ralph H. (Ron) Cook, became the executive director of SRL, adopting the pattern of staff relationship that LRY used, with a dual reporting relationship to the SRL Executive Committee and the UUA. The chair of the SRL board, R. Michael McKinlay, worked closely with Cook in his first year, for Cook's time had to be split between the field and the office. SRL's local chapters were always stronger than the continental group. Institutionally, SRL remained concerned with how to make itself more representative and how best to deal with the requirements of being the only Unitarian Universalist program for college students.

The Oxford Drug Crisis

The 1967 continental conference, held at the Western College for Women in Oxford, Ohio, marked a turning point in LRY. Domestic airlines had just instituted reduced youth fares, so attendance was high. The conference is remembered because drugs became a public issue for the first time at a continental conference. The resolution of that crisis would be a powerful experience for all concerned.

A small group of conferees discovered wild marijuana growing in the woods on the Oxford campus. At an early meeting of the whole conference, participants were urged not to harvest the marijuana, let alone smoke any of it. However, at the end of the week, four conferees were caught smoking. Greg Sweigert had just been elected the new president of LRY in an emotionally charged election, and this was his baptism of fire. In a lengthy meeting of LRY leaders, conference advisors, and the busted LRY members, it was decided to bring the matter up for the entire conference to talk about. That was the last night of what had been a very successful conference. The Beatles' new "Sgt. Pepper's Lonely Hearts Club Band" had been the soundtrack for the week. It was the "Summer of Love." People were full of stories of a wonderful renaissance happening among young people all over the country. How could a few LRY members possibly shatter that feeling of community by explicitly doing something that they had been told would threaten the very existence of LRY? It was hard to reconcile.

The conference was mired in contradictions and ambivalent feelings for a long time. A consensus finally emerged that the culprits would not be turned over to any authorities, and it was too late in the conference to ask them to leave. They would instead be asked to write a letter to the LRY board reflecting on why they had decided getting high at this conference was so important. A healing process had begun as a result of all this, but people went away with the feeling that things were never going to be quite the same again. Something had changed. Similar problems, and wider issues concerning the style of the American cultural presence within the IRF, plagued the IRF conference in Stanstead, Quebec, that same summer. Drug use as a public issue at conferences has remained a constant ethical and political challenge for youth leadership and youth advisors ever since.

LRY and the UUA

At the 1967 meetings, Dick Kossow outlined clearly to the LRY board the kind of financial crisis the UUA was facing. The board took a hard look at the Vanguard in Progress program, for it seemed apparent that the UUA would not be able to match any money that LRY raised. In a burst of denominational enthusiasm, the board decided to change the VIP program to a fundraising effort for the UUA. When it came time to choose a name for the program, everyone looked over Greg Sweigert's head to the poster that had hung behind him all during the LRY Executive Committee's meeting: a picture of W.C. Fields peering over a stacked poker hand. So began the "W.C. Fields Tripping Program," which managed to raise $5,000 from LRY local groups in one year for the UUA Annual Program Fund.

Those attending the 1967 continental conference and board meetings went back to their federations and local groups committed to serving as evangelists for UUA programs and fund-raising. The Sweigert committee traveled extensively and sent out posters, packets, and copies of *The Promethean*, edited by Ken Friedman (who was to become a well-known concept artist). The degree of involvement the local groups felt was reflected in the money they raised for the W.C. Fields fund. Sweigert was invited to present their check for $5,000 to UUA president Dana Greeley, with much ceremony, at the 1968 General Assembly in Cleveland. Unfortunately, Sweigert forgot the check in Boston, so when he ambled up on the platform to get the famous Greeley handshake, he was clutching in his hand an envelope containing only an IOU.

LRY attempted its first major political organizing within the denomination at the 1968 General Assembly. The General Assembly, held in Denver the previous year had seen but a smattering of LRY members. General Assemblies were still held in late May at that time, awkward timing for high school and college students since everyone was still in school. The interest in UUA financial and political affairs created by the W. C. Fields Tripping Program resulted in nearly thirty LRY members attending the

1968 GA in Cleveland, when the Black Affairs Council (BAC) controversy surfaced in the denomination. At a conference on the "Black Rebellion" in 1967 a caucus of African American UUs had emerged. Organizing as the Black Affairs Council, they sought UUA support for their economic development programs. BAC had asked for a one million-dollar budget allotment over four years (basing the figure on one dollar per year per Unitarian Universalist). The 1968 General Assembly approved their request. Most of the LRY delegates favored the request, but the role the LRY took at the assembly was that of peacemaker and court jester. To express affection for both UUA president Dana McLean Greeley and BAC chairman Hayward Henry, the youth waved "Dana loves Hayward" signs in the middle of tense debates on the Assembly floor.

By this time, LRY had developed an overt "hippie" image within the denomination. While running for the presidency of LRY that year, Larry Ladd remembers growing his beard out in order to look more hip. In spite of Larry's relatively conservative reputation, he had been elected as president at the continental conference in Santa Fe, New Mexico. The theme of that conference centered on marathon encounter group work. The whole conference divided into "cells," each led by one adult and one youth facilitator. The groups met together for the first part of the conference, and the remainder of the week was devoted to those groups examining their experiences of living in close communities. Similar themes had characterized other LRY conferences and camps that year; in particular, the Lake Geneva, Wisconsin, conference. A close and powerful group of LRY members emerged from that conference experience to burst onto the continental LRY scene over the next three years, electing six Executive Committee members.

In the fall of 1968, another style of conference programming emerged in a prototype conference held in Toronto. Its theme (or non-theme), "Do Your Own Shtick," began a trend of non-thematic conferences centered around individual workshops on a wide variety of topics. People from all over the East and the Midwest attended the "shtick conference," even though it was supposed to be an Eastern Canada Federation gathering.

Larry Ladd's Executive Committee was a diverse combination of people. In addition to Ladd—a calm, systematic administrator —the Committee included two full-time field trippers, a social actions director, and the youngest person ever elected to an LRY Executive Committee position (Deborah Mendelsohn, then sixteen). The LRY board also commissioned Sweigert to stay in Boston and edit a new LRY publication, The Nameless Newsprint, to replace the expensive *Promethean*. So with Kossow on full-time, the Boston office had three to five staff people on hand, and two to four in the field all year.

The 1968 board meetings, the last to follow the pattern established in the 1950s, took place in August in the New Mexico desert. The meetings were thrown into turmoil midweek by car radio reports of riots in the streets of Chicago. Many LRY members had left the continental conference the week before to join the Chicago protests at the Democratic National Convention. Worship services and anxious phone calls expressed deep concern.

The year 1968-1969 was crucial for LRY. The organization's character was changing dramatically from the bottom up. The local groups were dealing with all the new issues that "youth culture" had formed around: drug use, the human potential movement, a new sexual ethic, the draft, the war. The LRY Executive Committee became a more noticeable physical presence at the UUA's offices, day and night, sensing that they were in the eye of a hurricane and not sure in which direction to go.

The Nameless Newsprint became a major communication link between Boston and the local groups. The committee of 1968-1969 began the year focused on working with LRY locals and federations, but as the year wore on, UUA politics absorbed more of its energy. It was also becoming apparent that Kossow would not stay on as executive director much longer. Ladd took a much stronger role in the organization and administration of LRY during the latter part of the year.

In 1969, LRY found itself in the thick of an intensely political year for the UUA. The LRY Executive Committee members joined the coalition of white supporters, Full Funding for the Black Affairs Council (FULLBAC). It was clear that BAC funding would be challenged at the 1969 General Assembly in Boston. The UUA's program funds would be greatly reduced if the full funding commitment made in 1968 was sustained. In that UUA presidential election year, most candidates were paying attention to the youth presence within the denomination. In the spring of 1969, Robert Hohler, executive director of the Layman's League, held a sit-in fast in the lobby of 25 Beacon Street to protest the UUA's investment policies, and the Interdenominational Radical Caucus (IRC) occupied the Unitarian Universalist Service Committee (UUSC) building to protest the UUSC's project work in Vietnam. The IRC drew much support from local LRY and SRL members in Boston.

While all this was going on, the LRY leadership was formulating its own plans for the 1969 General Assembly. LRY's institutional situation at the time was at a crossroads. Kossow would be leaving at the year's end. LRY had continued to grow in size, even beyond the big spurt of Leon Hopper's years. Yet neither the UUA nor its predecessors had increased funds for youth programming since LRY's formation in 1954. The LRY board directly controlled about ten thousand dollars of its own budget, which it obtained in endowment interest and federation dues. Its remaining funds were held by the Department of Education and paid out for professional staff salaries and travel and office needs. The LRY-SRL endowment fund was held in the UUA General Investment Fund and invested in politically questionable stocks. The 1968-1969 committee had more full-time LRY members than ever before, and they felt much closer to the program needs of rank-and-file LRY membership. They were prepared to risk trying to gain full control of LRY financial resources and build a totally youth-run program.

Larry Ladd laid out the philosophy behind LRY's new political stance in an article in *The Nameless Newsprint* entitled "Bitter Brooklyn." His far-reaching statement outlined the liberation issues high school students in general were concerned with. In April 1969 in Huntington, Long Island, the 1968-1969 Executive Committee and all candidates for office met to formulate a youth agenda for General Assembly.

The group decided to mount a major effort at getting youth delegates to General Assembly. LRY would demand UUA funding of $100,000 for youth programs and complete control of its own endowment fund. The group decided not to hire another executive director. To save money on board meetings and to help get people to the General Assembly, they agreed to hold the continental board meetings immediately after General Assembly instead of at the continental conference later that summer.

It was an embattled UUA administration that received the youth agenda demands. Reactions in the churches ranged from disbelief and hostility, through indifference, to cautious support.

Nevertheless, a compromise was reached without taking the issue to the GA floor. Following a cost-accounting study of LRY and SRL, Raymond Hopkins, the UUA vice president, pointed out that nearly $100,000 was already being spent annually on the two programs, counting in all staff salaries, expenses, office costs, rent for the office at 25 Beacon Street, and the Billings Lecture Fund, which SRL was controlling and using to send UU troubadour and minister Ric Masten around the country. Hopkins offered to remove LRY and SRL from the Department of Education budget, grant them their money directly, and release the endowment from the General Investment Fund, if both organizations would pay the UUA directly for all the services they used. The LRY members agreed. Those in SRL did too, albeit more cautiously. Ron Cook was also resigning his position to join the Starr King School faculty, leaving SRL in the same position as LRY.

Though the youth agenda had been resolved to some extent, the momentum that had been built up was applied to the rest of the business before the General Assembly. About one hundred young people participated in the 1969 GA, including some sixty-two delegates. The young people and IRC group established a

small encampment on the mezzanine floor of Boston's Statler
Hilton Hotel. The first Youth Caucus was hard to miss in their ply-
wood geodesic dome. The youth leadership conducted informa-
tional meetings for the youth delegates where representatives of all
sides of the issues before the Assembly had a chance to explain
their positions, particularly various groups that had formed
around the issue of Black Affairs Council funding.

Youth delegates became an active part of the FULLBAC coalition at General Assembly. When the GA delegates voted against
moving the vote on BAC funding to the front of the agenda, youth
delegates joined BAC delegates in physically seizing the microphones. Some people suggested that the youth delegates were
being manipulated by BAC members. Actually, although the youth
were kept informed of the floor strategy the Black Caucus was
planning, they were never overtly pressured into joining them in
any planned action. The night before the issue came to a head, the
BAC leadership and their LRY-age members briefed the Youth
Caucus leadership about exactly what alternatives were being considered. The LRY delegates had known of the plan for BAC
spokesmen to seize the microphones. BAC representatives had ad-
vised the youth that the degree to which they supported that action was up to them. When the Assembly refused to change the
agenda to allow the BAC question to be considered immediately,
each youth delegate who responded by blocking access to the microphones acted out of his or her own conscience.

When Rev. Jack Mendelsohn came to the podium and announced that the Black Caucus had left the assembly, most of the
youth delegation decided—unexpectedly and spontaneously—to
walk out too, many feeling as though they were walking out of the
denomination altogether. The delegates who had left began meeting at the Arlington Street Church. As the day wore on, however,
it became apparent that the Assembly must seek common ground.
The Youth Caucus decided to seek it in a worship service.

That evening after the walkout, people holding all perspec-
tives on the issue attended the LRY service in the Arlington Street

church. All joined in singing the LRY hymn, "We Would Be One," twice through at the closing. It was not a solution, but it was a beginning. It was important to stay together. When Dana Greeley came personally to the Arlington Street church to ask them to come back, the delegates returned to the main assembly body. LRY members dumped boxes of balloons from the balcony over the delegates' heads as they reentered the hall.

When the vote on BAC funding was finally reconsidered by the reunited General Assembly, the youth delegates voted nearly unanimously in favor of the commitment to BAC. The Assembly vote was close, but the motion carried.

The 1969 General Assembly felt like one great public victory for the leaders of the Youth Caucus, but it would be the prelude to a series of disappointments and defeats.

⸮

Attention:
(but you know that's only part of it)
We had a space that was ours only—
enlightening leaded windows, grey stone walls
a pervasive solidity, cool and comfortable.
We painted it black.

The Skunch Room:

Where-in we re-writ All of Us in Wonderland.
Seven levels, to be precise,
all in a room which was probably not larger
than twelve by twenty.
Seven levels built from old lumber carried up
from the inner basement.
The room next to the crypt for the Skunch room
rested peacefully and in its raucous moments also,
upon a shadowed catacomb holy and mysterious.

Damn right a place to love and hide!

The shelter of our confessions,
our sanctuary.

It was just the same as this moment then,
only faster. We were so much more desperate to age.
"There is no such thing as retreat,
there is only strategic withdrawal."
(The ROTC Handbook)

If we learned to love and hide and recuperate,
we also learned to struggle in the world.
For we have a vision and we are not the only ones.
Out of old lumber and resting upon
the integrity of a common dream,

we have set out to build.

To you who are fearful:
I am fearful also. The awkward dance we danced
so laughable, so exquisite,
searching for balance, learning to rely on breath.
It is not beyond you to sense the ecstasy
as well as the danger.

High drama is worthy of attention.
I tell you the church is the womb.
It is the place of birth and dedication.
It gave us a place to love.
We will be true to its
holy intention.

Rob Eller-Isaacs
Chicago, Illinois

What has been important to me about being in the IRF? First and
most of all learning to accept other people's way of life. Can you

imagine that I was embarrassed when an American friend who stayed with me made himself a super sandwich at my table? It's not that I couldn't afford such an expense, but I was brought up in the years of scarcity just after World War II in the Netherlands, a country that has known many a hungry winter. Moreover, we are taught to be modest when we are guests in another's home. I've known many other situations in which my childhood (or deeply anchored and culturally determined) convictions were shaken by friends from other countries.

There also exist all sorts of differences in thinking between the various language groups. I attended a workshop once on "language" at a conference, and while the English-speaking people were eager to begin, a French person asked: "Are we talking about langue, language, parole, or mot?" In other words, the French think in more precise categories for the concept of "language." I always found it amusing that the constitution of IRF (published in both English and German) contains the provision, "In case of doubt, the English version shall rule!" And English phrases are often so ambiguous!

Discovering my own values was a striking aspect of going to IRF for me. It provided an opportunity to build long-lasting relationships. Having been at eleven summer IRF conferences, I can testify that IRF is able to create a support group for youth and young adults from many parts of the world.

One thing is certain: I experienced many firsts in my life at IRF meetings, which I started attending in 1966. I made my first and only macramé belt, played a simulation game on world development for the first time, had my first women's discussion in IRF, enjoyed and felt comfortable in a worship service as I'd never done before, stayed up to watch the sunrise, ate my first lobster, and stood for the first time in a circle holding many friends and singing the following chants that summarize for me the meaning of the International Religious Fellowship:

wearing my long wing feathers
 as I fly
 I circle around
 the boundaries of the Earth

Listen listen listen
to my heart's song
I will never forget you
I will never forsake you

Lucie Meijer
Utrecht, The Netherlands

The New Community

THE SHELL-SHOCKED LRY Board of Trustees that met in Concord, Massachusetts, after the 1969 General Assembly faced the responsibility of carving up a $45,000 budget for the first time. To make matters worse, that year's elections were a painful process, with multiple candidates for each office. Robert Isaacs was elected president, but no candidate received a majority of votes for three of the positions on the new Executive Committee. Those were finally filled through appointments, largely from among the pool of losing candidates.

Money Problems

The 1969 LRY board was feisty, with many federation representatives advocating a "states' rights" position. Rather than pay dues at the continental level anymore, they wanted a piece of LRY's new-found wealth for the regional level. The first budget drawn up, based on everyone's stated needs and the programs the Executive Committee had in mind, totaled $62,000. The difficult process of budget-trimming began and continued for several years. Halfway through the 1969-1970 year the UUA cut the LRY budget by nearly one-third, down to $32,000, as the new UUA president, Robert West, began drastic surgery on the denomination's finances. So, much of the work done by the LRY board in Concord would be in vain.

The board met later that summer in Seabeck, Washington, at the continental conference, where more budget squabbling took interminable time and alienated the Executive Committee from the board. In contrast, the LRY conference proved quite successful. With the theme "Stewed Rhubarb" — essentially a non-theme—it was the first continental conference to operate on the workshops-only model. A beautiful madness surrounded it. The Sahili Federation Executive Committee won the prize offered for the most original conference arrival by driving in atop a full-sized mobile calliope.

Meanwhile, at their 1969 continental conference in Colorado Springs, Colorado, Student Religious Liberals underwent significant restructuring. Ron Cook had left and no new professional staff person would be hired. SRL was beginning to see its constituency as wider than just college students and wanted to try a budgeting approach that would allow the maximum opportunity for constituents to start locally based projects on their own initiative. Reflecting these changes, the organization expanded its name to "SRL, A Free Religious Fellowship."

The 1969-1970 LRY Executive Committee was the first to set up shop full-time with an apartment in Boston. The group worked with a hired secretary and an adult advisor rather than any new executive director. By January, 1970, their high hopes and attempts at tight organization were crumbling around them. A variety of things contributed to the decay. The LRY board had been merciless in its budget allotment for the Executive Committee's personal needs, so they were living in a slum apartment in Cambridge on stipends of fifty dollars per month. Disagreements with the LRY Board of Trustees were a constant grind. After the UUA cut the budget in November, the Executive Committee could not agree on how to realign priorities. In February 1970 committee members agreed to work independently on their program responsibilities without consensus or formal meetings as a whole group until summer.

The LRY leadership was also deeply discouraged by UUA politics. The financial crisis that UUA president Robert West had been forced to deal with affected all departments and everyone's morale. The reality of funding the commitment to the Black Affairs Council loomed large in the challenges West had to face. The UUA administration would recommend, and the board would ultimately approve, that BAC funding be cut, despite the General Assembly votes of 1968 and 1969. LRY leaders had remained involved in the work of the Fellowship for Renewal (FFR), the ongoing group created out of the 1969 GA to advocate for the BAC agenda and to take up other issues of cultural and political renewal in the association. Wayne Arnason and John Gibbons worked with Rev. Bob Wheatly, Ann Raynolds, and Robert Hohler to create and staff an FFR office. They organized a public witness of sixty UUs from around the continent at the UUA Board of Trustees meeting in January 1970 where the recommendation to reduce BAC funding was passed.

For its own part, LRY had decided to go beyond mere political support and make the firmest possible commitment to the Black Affairs Council. When UUA funds for its economic empowerment programs were cut, BAC went directly to churches and UU organizations for funding through a bond issue. LRY pledged one-half of the endowment fund it now controlled to the BAC Bond program, and, later that year, became the first of many UU organizations and congregations to buy the bonds.

As the 1970 General Assembly in Seattle, Washington, approached, the Executive Committee began pulling itself back together. LRY and the Fellowship for Renewal coordinated General Assembly plans, hoping to draw progressive youth and adults to GA in large numbers. The expense of attending GA in a fancy hotel was an obstacle for youth and lower-income adults. An old hotel in Seattle that was being operated as a hippie hostel was located, and LRY rented the whole building for $100 for GA week. They advertised free "crash space" at the "beautiful" Fremont Hotel for anyone who wanted it, with private rooms at minimal cost. The Seattle press headlined a story about the UU convention as "A Tale of Two Hotels." Late in the week, the Seattle Fire Department closed the hotel for fire code violations, and all the

Unitarian Universalists staying there had to find space with friends or real hotel rooms. At the main convention hotel, LRY's major evening program was a dance, featuring Big Brother and the Holding Company (minus Janis Joplin, who had died earlier in the year). The cultural gap between most of the GA's adult and youth delegates had never felt wider.

Yet many of LRY's political goals were achieved at that General Assembly. LRY Executive Committee members spearheaded the effort to place on the agenda and support resolutions on legalization of marijuana and civil rights for homosexual people. The Assembly approved both. The resolution on civil rights for homosexuals was a landmark—the first public statement by the Unitarian Universalist Association on gay rights. LRY also received a commitment from the Planning Committee and board that every effort would be made to continue to have General Assemblies in late June so students could attend.

In so many ways, the Youth Agenda goals set for 1968 through 1970 had been fulfilled, but that satisfaction was embittered by the constant threat of continuing budget cuts and uncertainty among LRY's leadership as to direction.

New Leadership

During the 1970s, LRY leaders went through a trial and error process of finding the best way to function under self-leadership within the precarious new relationship with the UUA. The 1969 change was major, and it would be three years before organizational roles and patterns were established that could provide some degree of stability and efficiency within the leadership. The top-heavy, eight-member 1970-1971 committee, with Larry Brown as president, fragmented as badly as had the one before it. Four members were asked to resign at mid-year to bring the leadership down to a financially manageable and responsible group.

In the fall of 1970, the UUA established a committee of its board as a funnel for the youth program monies. Leon Hopper, by then a UUA board member, was appointed as a representative to this new Youth-Adult Committee, along with Julie Underwood. A long process of trust-building followed to create an effective working relationship between this board committee and the LRY executives. The Youth-Adult Committee gradually developed into a valuable advisory board for UU youth programming.

In 1971, Charles B. (Chuck) Rosene was elected president of a four-member Executive Committee, serving with Molly Monahan, Kim Yasutake, and Rick Reiser. This committee established itself in relative stability and began to function in a more productive collective fashion than its two predecessors. Members agreed to remain Boston-based and to try to bring LRY's focus back to relevant programming for local groups. The LRY office was re-organized, with mutually satisfactory diplomatic relations with the denomination restored.

One major task for the Executive Committee and its successors was to respond to the changes that had taken place in high-school-age culture, as reflected in LRY local groups. Developing program materials for high school students had become more difficult than ever.

The 1971-1972 Executive Committee's first "new" programming initiative made use of old ones: It reviewed and "recycled" the 1960s LRY programs that continued to seem relevant. Some were reprinted, some were adapted, and others were completely rewritten to fit the needs of contemporary LRY members.

The New Community was a program approach designed by the 1972-1973 Executive Committee, consisting of Gale Pingel, Claudia Nalven, Holly Horn, and John Byrne. It offered a wide range of program suggestions for LRY local groups that were designed to help them develop an image of themselves as a caring, extended family based on a concept of religious community that furthers personal liberation. Taking advantage of the skills and approaches to adult programming within the UUA Department of Education, the program was based on a vision of what a meaningful LRY local group could be. It furthermore incorporated a badly needed feminist perspective.

This Executive Committee also decided to abandon the hierarchical model of leadership, which its members saw as inconsistent with their political philosophy. So Gale Pingel served as the last president of LRY. Once the 1972-1973 committee retired, a new system of directorships was established. Each Executive Committee member was to be elected to a position bearing a specific job description. The committee would attempt to make broad policy decisions collectively.

The 1973-1974 Executive Committee (Adam Auster, Peter Nalven, Paula Rose, and Matthew Easton) revised LRY's constitution and bylaws to reflect its changing character. The committee's major programming innovation was the initiation of *People Soup*, a newspaper to be mailed directly to all LRY members up to eight times a year. This was the first consistent program publication to come out of LRY since the *Nameless Newsprint* folded in 1970. Initially, the committee tried to put *People Soup* out on a subscription basis, using a special grant from the Youth-Adult Committee to support the first few issues. Beginning in 1974, it was mailed free to every Unitarian Universalist church, a large list of LRY members, and anyone else who wanted it. In 1975, Bev Treumann initiated *Cream of People Soup*, a compilation of the best local group program ideas from several issues into one paper.

A formal ongoing model for the General Assembly Youth Caucus within the UUA was created in 1975 under the leadership of LRY director Lara Stahl. The Youth Caucus was intended to be a rallying point for all UU youth attending the annual General Assembly. Though organized by LRY, the caucus was also intended to serve youth attending GA who were unaffiliated with LRY. By raising scholarship funds and providing information and issue-based discussion sessions, the caucus began to provide a valuable home base for all young people finding their way through the large and often confusing GA process.

Almost all LRY executive committees of the 1970s experienced continual tension arising from the day-to-day grind of coworkers living together. Several changes of apartments, which gradually increased the available living space for the four executives, temporarily alleviated the difficult situation. However, extra space would all too soon be filled by the inevitable army of traveling LRY members who would come to stay for a few hours, a few days, or a few months. The creation in 1976 of a month-long internship program for LRY members interested in trying out the Executive Committee experience added to the crowding. Between 1969 and 1979, only three executive committees survived their full-year term without the resignation of at least one member. Nevertheless, the people who served as "Tacos" (the nickname for the Executive Committee members or interns) during those years remember them vividly as challenging and growing times.

The lack of continuity from one executive committee to another multiplied the enormity of the task facing the new group arriving in Boston each fall. The committees involved in this transition in 1974 tried to remedy the situation by choosing one member of the outgoing group to stay on in the office into the fall of the new fiscal year to help the incoming group. Then, in 1977, the LRY board decided to stagger the Executive Committee terms, electing two in the winter and two in the summer, in order to maximize continuity within the leadership.

LRY in Decline

By 1974, Liberal Religious Youth was clearly suffering a serious decline on the regional and local levels. Some critics were quick to blame the decline in the size and shape of local programs on the radical youth leadership ideology that had emerged at the turn of the decade. Most districts within the UUA included one or more churches that had suffered property damage, inconvenience to members, or emotional casualties connected to LRY events that had been completely youth-run and run badly. Despite its long history within the association, the ideology of a predominantly youth-run program had become identified with drug use, unconventional costumes, and greater sexual freedom at younger ages. Teenagers, as well as parents, who did not embrace this culture felt uncomfortable about getting involved with local LRY groups. Some churches tried to remedy this situation by dropping the name "Liberal Religious Youth" and setting up youth groups that were led by adults and insulated from contact with regional and continental LRY programs.

Indeed, a fire had been burning to generate all this smoke. Youth leadership on the continental level often downgraded the efficiency and outreach of the denomination's central office for youth programming. Reasons included the lifestyle and work process that adolescents collectively adopted when they came to Boston for a year to do the job, and youth leaders' lack of expertise with respect to efficient office procedures. Another problem, however, was UU church leaders' unwillingness to cooperate with and respond to youth leaders' efforts to influence local programming.

Factors beyond the control of both youth and adult leaders also played a major part in this decline. A typical member of LRY in 1974 had been born between 1957 and 1959 and entered adolescence in the 1970s. The baby-boom wave of young people that had washed over the denomination in the 1960s was leveling out. Fewer adolescents were available to join any youth group. Furthermore, youth culture in the 1970s no longer had the sharp focus of the late 1960s. The frontiers for adolescents of five years earlier had become the new LRY playgrounds. Politically and sociologically, there was less unity and no clear direction for youth culture.

Unitarian Universalism was also declining over this period. Membership was dropping from the high levels achieved in the early 1960s. In addition to fewer adolescent children among church families, fewer families in the 1970s were bringing their children up through church school. Many of our churches, especially in urban areas, increasingly drew single people. This fact made one phenomenon in some of our churches particularly curious, the tendency to regard LRY members whose parents were not Unitarian Universalist as "outsiders" instead of "converts" who were making a connection with the levels of institutional Unitarian Universalism that they could most easily relate to.

Drawing from a smaller membership base, discouraged by frustration and hostility from many adults, and lacking a transmission of leadership skills and motivation from one generation of LRY members to the next, many LRY regions, federations, and local groups simply dried up. Our churches were often glad to see them go.

The SRL Land Rush

Although LRY had made a relatively successful transition into the mechanics of running its own program, Student Religious Liberals never really did. The role of the SRL executive secretary in Boston, Joanne Powers, was reduced to that of a newsletter editor and channel of communication between board members. The new board members of SRL lost interest in doing the kind of field work and correspondence necessary to keep in touch with their eroding base of campus groups.

In the winter of 1971, the board decided to fire Powers and install one of its own members in Boston as the executive secretary. At that time, the group also became interested in an idea that would consume the time and energy of three successive "generations" of SRL members. The idea was to invest the SRL share of the endowment fund for youth programming in land and establish a community of SRL representatives who would function as role models and coordinate the SRL organization. Leaders who got excited about the idea over the years were long on dreams and good intentions but short on practical know-how and long-term commitment.

The first group that tried to pull together a land investment fell apart due to greed and lack of trust among board members. Citing mismanagement of funds, the UUA's Youth-Adult Committee decided to cut the SRL program budget back from $25,000 to a bare institutional minimum of $7,000. A younger college-age group picked up the pieces and tried to bring the organization back to life. They hired Wayne Arnason, then a student at Harvard Divinity School and a former LRY leader, to run their office.

At the 1973 SRL continental conference at DeBenneville Pines in California, a new group of members caught land fever and began the hunt all over again. This group looked thoroughly at pieces of land in California, Florida, and New England before settling on a property in upstate New York near Saratoga Springs. At the 1974 continental conference in Colorado, they reached the decision to buy. "Pioneers" volunteered to be the first to live on the property and get it into shape before winter set in. However, when the group met all together on the actual property to seal the deal, they realized the enormity of the task facing them, and decided they lacked the stamina to see it through. This group of SRL members continued to function for another year, but the collapse of the land plans destroyed the momentum it had generated.

SRL Changes Direction

The institutional structure of SRL languished until a new group picked up the pieces in 1976. By then, the campus SRL groups had all but vanished. The organization had become an alumni association of old LRY members who wanted to continue the friendships and conference experiences that had been so important in their LRY years, and a network of young adults with varying connections to Unitarian Universalism who were interested in alternative lifestyles and communal living. The group that took over the SRL structure in 1976 decided to make explicit the fact that the group was no longer the denomination's college-age program in any real sense. Adopting the name Communities for Study and Action (CSA), the group decided not to ask the UUA for continued funding but to proceed in its own direction. In the summer of 1978, CSA dissolved what was left of the institutional structure of Student Religious Liberals and returned the SRL portion of the endowment fund to LRY.

The SRL story over the 1970s was not entirely about decline

and dissolution. For seven summers after the structural changes of 1969 and 1970, its annual conferences drew average attendance of seventy-five to one hundred. The program continued to provide a community within Unitarian Universalism for hundreds of young adults who had been highly motivated by their LRY experiences but now had no place to put all that energy. For a smaller group, the land projects proved an invaluable learning experience. SRL was the only program for young adults connected to Unitarian Universalism during the 1970s, when the association had no money or will to support any other kind of program. CSA continued that thread of young adult networking until the early 1980s, when UUA staff launched the next serious effort to rebuild young adult programs.

During the 1970s, SRL members also became more deeply involved with the International Religious Fellowship, thanks to contacts between LRY, SRL, and IRF leaders. In 1972 the SRL and IRF held their conferences jointly on Cape Cod, Massachusetts. Prior to those conferences, the Americans organized and led a two-week tour of the Eastern United States and Canada, which helped to build friendships and community. In 1975 the Americans offered their European friends a three-week tour of western Canada and the United States, culminating in a long bus ride back across America to the IRF and SRL conferences in western Massachusetts.

With the shutdown of SRL operations in 1978, formal contacts with IRF evaporated. IRF relied on old friends and LRY leaders to keep Americans informed about its programs and activities.

IRF and the Art of Living Together

International Religious Fellowship had continued to thrive in the late 1960s, although Albert Schweitzer College did not. The college moved from Churwalden to a site near Lausanne, Switzerland, in 1965, and closed shortly afterward, following unsuccessful fundraising campaigns.

In 1966, IRF became a full-member group of the International Association for Religious Freedom. During the 1970s, as IARF changed from a scholarly conclave to a "world council" of liberal religious churches, IRF members became much more involved in its congresses and activities. While only a handful of IRF people attended the IARF Congress in Heidelberg in 1972, IARF's 1972 Montreal Congress welcomed a busload of IRF members who had ridden up to participate following their own conference in Massachusetts. The 1978 IRF conference was held in conjunction with the IARF Congress and had over sixty young people in attendance.

In the late 1960s and early 1970s, IRF conference themes and styles of programming moved from abstract topics to more personal issues. This was partly due to the influence of the American LRY and SRL members who had become involved in IRF. However, the youth culture of the 1960s was an international phenomenon, leading European member groups to seek deeper levels for conference themes. The 1971 theme was "Mind Expansion." The 1973 conference became the scene of fierce controversy regarding the respect individual IRF members awarded religious symbols, especially symbols of Christianity. The 1974 conference centered on "The Art of Living Together," with encounter groups and sensitivity trainings. In 1975, the conference, held in America, dealt with sexism on both personal and political levels.

The IRF/SRL tours in America cemented many important friendships and offered an opportunity for young religious liberals from Europe to see America from the inside out. The European group reciprocated with a 1978 tour of Europe for American friends following the IRF-IARF Congress. The first IRF tour of Japan took place in the summer of 1975.

Liberal religious movements in Europe during the 1970s experienced the same decline in young-adult involvement that the Unitarian Universalist Association was suffering. By the end of the decade, IRF faced a real question about whether it could remain an organization of member groups or would become a society of individual members. During the 1980s IRF held some modest conference events and reunions. The International Association for Religious Freedom (IARF) and the UUA staff organized international youth events in Japan and India in the early part of the decade and IARF conferences continued to encourage a youth presence, but by the 1990s IRF had ceased to function as a distinct young adult member group of IARF.

The SCOYP Report

By late 1975, concern was growing about the lack of adequate support for youth programming in the Unitarian Universalist Association. In April, 1976, members of the continental LRY Executive Committee, acutely aware of their own and the UUA's inadequacies, asked for time on the UUA board's agenda. Acting on LRY's suggestion, as presented by Jennifer Shaw, the UUA board voted to establish a Special Committee on Youth Programs (SCOYP), with the following charge:

> . . . to study the existing youth programs in the denomination, including LRY, and to make proposals, including budget proposals, to the Board as to the best ways for the UUA to develop, offer and support programs for youth generally of high school age. . . . The Board agrees that the budget recommendations of the Committee should include alternatives.

The committee of seven, three youth and four adults, consisted of retiring LRY Executive Committee member Shaw, former LRY executive director Leon Hopper, director of religious education Elaine Smith from First Unitarian Church in Seattle, psychologist Tom Greenspon, UU seminarian Anne Heller (a former Girl Scout executive), LRY youth Kim DeRidder, and Eric Joselyn, who was active in a UU youth program unaffiliated with LRY. SCOYP also consulted with Dr. Gisela Knopka, director of the Center for Youth Development and Research at the University of Minnesota. SCOYP met four times, spending over fifteen months compiling information and examining youth programs throughout the

UU denomination. It is interesting to compare what the 1977 committee found to be the scope of UU local youth programs with Leon Hopper's 1963 statistics. In 1963, in his final report as LRY executive director, Hopper had reported that at least 450 active LRY groups held some degree of affiliation with the organization through its 33 active federations. Using the UUA's statistics from its annual questionnaire, SCOYP reported 380 high school-age youth groups, with more of those identified as high school groups (225) than as LRY groups (155). These numbers are not entirely clear, however, since the report indicated that some groups functioned as LRY-style programs but avoided the name because it had a stigma associated with it, while other groups used the name but had no relationship to other levels of the program, such as participation in federation or continental-level conferences or programs.

The SCOYP report did not detail the status of LRY federations, but minutes would indicate that at best, half the number reported in 1963 had survived. The report acknowledged the existence of a number of summer camps and conferences for youth. Although these were promoted and sponsored by youth leaders, they had no formal relationship to either LRY or any church or church organization.

The cover page of the committee's twenty-five-page report, submitted in November 1977 offers a quote that indicates the degree to which the committee expected its conclusions would generate controversy: "The turtle only advances by sticking its neck out." Over the next two years, that controversy focused on whether to implement the SCOYP report's final recommendations for reorganization and if so, how. Lost in that discussion, and in the SCOYP report's place in youth movement history, are some of the best summary statements of the goals and guiding philosophies that have underlaid UU youth programming. Among several statements of the committee's positions about the denomination's objectives for youth programming, we find these paragraphs:

> Young adults are searching for meaning in life and for personal identity. They seek continuity, power, and a responsi-

ble place in the world. Because of extended adolescence and the dissolving nature of contemporary community, the search and the space to find personal answers are increasingly disparate. UUA program goals for youth must be responsive to the needs of youth, or youth will continue to drop out and vanish. UU societies should provide meaningful programs to their youth in a consistent way. A program for youth needs to offer a safe space for transition and passage; it needs to offer experience with real power; an opportunity to develop a personal religious philosophy, and significant meaningful work. The programs should foster a commitment to the larger UU body, celebrate potential for continuous growth and change throughout life, and affirm the questioning stance of adolescence. If a program or group works well, a family-type bonded atmosphere will prevail.

Adults working with youth must be authentic, secure in their adulthood, and able to stand by their principles without trying to "program" young people. Adults should be able to facilitate self-exploration, the facing of difficult decisions, and the examination of the consequences of decisions on the part of youth in an open-growth producing fashion. Adults should set limits with respect to their rights as human beings and should be ready to confront issues related to this at every opportunity. They should realize that abuse of sexuality and intoxicating chemicals by adolescents is frequently a purposeful attempt at control of self and others, or is a goal directed in some other way, and that these issues should be explored . . . . Manipulative personal involvements between group advisors and youth are divisive and destructive of the group's efforts at personal empowerment . . . .

Adults working with youth should be members of the UU community. They should be familiar with the goals of the church or fellowship and see the young people as valuable members of the UU community. The denomination has the responsibility to adults working with youth to provide training and support that will enable them to carry out their charge.

Youth programs in our churches and fellowships deserve and are entitled to the same kind of personal, financial, and staff support that other activities receive.

Despite the considerable understanding that SCOYP showed for the goals and needs of UU youth programming, LRY's youth leadership had difficulty accepting the recommendations it made for meeting those goals and needs. SCOYP had reached two major conclusions: First, the status quo was inadequate and a disservice to youth. Second, the adult church had massively abdicated its responsibility in regard to youth programming. The report analyzed the reasons for these two problems and proceeded to make several alternative recommendations for action, with projected budgets attached to each.

The most substantial recommendation was that the resident Executive Committee of LRY be replaced by an Office of Youth Programs, staffed by an adult staff person and a secretary. Liberal Religious Youth would continue to be funded for specific programming, but not for housing its elected leaders in a central office within the UUA structure. The committee also recommended a restructuring of the denomination's Youth-Adult Committee and a denomination-wide dialogue over two years, starting at the local and district levels and culminating in a funded intergenerational conference on the continental level. The goal of the dialogue was not expressed as creation of a new UU youth organization. Indeed, SCOYP's recommendations pointed away from an organization for youth and focused instead on programs that would support local churches and their youth groups.

Many of the leaders, members, and friends of LRY felt they had been made the scapegoats for a complex of problems that led to decline of the youth program. That common placebo for all denominational ills, a staff person in an office, seemed to many critics like a particularly tired and inappropriate solution. On the other side, many in the denomination felt that some dramatic action had to be taken to pull the youth program out of the doldrums. They could not see either the LRY Executive Committee or the UUA board as an effective agent for such action.

UUA president Paul Carnes was unwilling to push the UUA board toward immediate implementation of the SCOYP recommendations in light of the controversy surrounding them. LRY's 1977-1978 Executive Committee, consisting of Shelley Cantril, Susan Buis, Abbe Bjorkland, and Barbara Dykes, proved a particularly effective, hard-working committee. Its members' efforts to rally opposition to the SCOYP recommendations resulted in a nine-month moratorium on any decision in order to encourage further response from the local level.

Churches, LRY groups, district youth-adult committees, and religious education committees all held discussions and forums about SCOYP's recommendations. Their responses reflected the continuing polarization within the Unitarian Universalist Association as to whether Liberal Religious Youth was adequate to continue as the denomination's only youth program. Meanwhile, President Carnes had suffered a recurrence of the cancer with which he had lived for some years and was near death by the winter of 1979.

The continental Youth-Adult Committee that met in March of 1979 was polarized. A majority (mostly youth) endorsed a recommendation that UUA continue to fund Liberal Religious Youth in full, while hiring a half-time staff person as a consultant on youth programming to supplement its work. A minority of the committee members endorsed an alternative recommendation, drafted by the committee's chair, Rev. Bruce Southworth, suggesting that the UUA hire a full-time consultant on youth programs and not continue to fund a full-time LRY staff of high school-age people in Boston.

The UUA board rejected the majority report of the Youth-Adult Committee and endorsed instead the minority, setting the scene for a floor fight during the budget debate at the 1979 General Assembly in East Lansing, Michigan.

Following the death of UUA president Paul Carnes, Rev. O. Eugene Pickett was elected president of the association. Although committed to a new full-time staff person for youth programs, he was open to a compromise that would allow the LRY leadership to continue working full-time as well. An amendment to the Youth Caucus resolution on the budget, proposed by Rev. Wayne Arnason and adopted by the General Assembly, opened the way for President Pickett and the LRY leadership to negotiate a compromise, allowing both staffing options to continue for at least a year. In September 1979 Pickett offered Arnason the opportunity to become the first adult in ten years to work full-time in the area of UU youth programming. He accepted.

The Unitarian church in Birmingham, Michigan, played a major role in helping me develop into the person I am today. The community I grew up in was fairly conservative and I really did not fit in. The Unitarian Church and its youth groups were a sanctuary for me. A safe place to be myself, express my self, share understanding with others, and to develop a personal and distinctive style that has served me well all of my life.

In 1976, Grant Drutchas, Cathy Schwing, and I chose to start a new youth group at Birmingham Unitarian Church instead of going into LRY for a very simple reason. Grant's father forbade him to join LRY because his older brother began smoking in LRY. The three of us had been together and played leadership roles in our junior high youth group. More often than not, Grant had been president, and we couldn't bear the thought of being split up.

We couldn't figure out what to call the group, so as a stopgap measure, Grant came up with GUSH (Great Un-named Senior Highers). I believe "Un-named" was later changed to "Unitarian." We started out with a small core group and all became very close. Others gradually realized we had something special going on, and we began to grow steadily.

Our congregation as a whole was not initially enthusiastic about our group. (I was told years later that the congregation had an adversarial relationship with the LRY.) However, we had a series of amazing advisors and support from two great directors of religious education (Jean Mehlenbacher and Pat Schwing) and the minister (Bob Marshall). In our second year, when we asked to do a Sunday service, we met real resistance. We felt we had a lot to contribute and say. We wanted to be part of the larger congregation so we persisted and were finally given a Sunday.

We worked on the service for four months. We planned every detail, performed our own music, wrote our own speaking parts, and practiced till we felt it was right. The service went beautifully. I believe it fundamentally changed the perception of the congregation toward our group. The "Youth Sunday" service became a yearly tradition.

I am kind of amazed that the little group we started is still in existence. We didn't set out with any sort of ambitions. We just wanted a safe place to be together where we could be ourselves.

Kevin Appleton
Birmingham, MI

Looking back on it now as a parent, I have a somewhat different perspective. When I was thirteen, I used to ride four hours in the bed of a truck to conferences—just laying there all wrapped around each other watching the sky go by. Now, I wouldn't dream of letting my seven-year-old ride in the car without being in a safety seat in the back seat. Tommy James used to hitchhike across country to attend LRY board meetings at fifteen. In the 1970s we used to plan our own conferences, inviting whatever speakers we wanted. We had people from Planned Parenthood do a women-only workshop where we all looked at our own cervixes. We had scientists from Jet Propulsion Laboratory come talk about God. We had meditation services with a full hour of "om"ing. We had Vision Quests creating paths and poetry in the forests. We were terribly afraid that too many adults might turn the whole thing too bloody serious. Yeah, we wanted to save the world, but we wanted to savor it too. UU adults tended to forget about the savoring part.

Caprice Young
Los Angeles, California

Looking for Common Ground

REV. WAYNE ARNASON, in conjunction with the LRY Executive Committee, expanded the SCOYP recommendation for a continental dialogue into a proposal for a continental youth assembly that would bring together youth and adult delegates from across North America to re-imagine Unitarian Universalist youth programs. The UUA Board of Trustees accepted the proposal, and the conference, titled "Common Ground," was held from August 10 to 15, 1981, at Carleton College in Northfield, Minnesota. The UUA, the North Shore Unitarian Society Veatch Program, the Unitarian Sunday School Society, and the Universalist Church School Union funded this unique assembly of 275 delegates.

Hopes and Anxieties

O. Eugene Pickett began his term as the fourth president of the UUA in 1979 and Common Ground fit into his priorities for his terms in office:

> Our religious education program was declining in members, as were youth programs. I'm not sure that the pressure was to shut down LRY as much as it was to integrate youth programs in the UUA structure, and to get more adult involvement in the decision-making and program planning. The kids were feeling partially victimized, but they were also rec-

ognizing that they were frustrated that they couldn't provide the necessary programs.

An advance-publicity conference brochure, "The Dozen Most Frequently Asked Questions About Common Ground," outlined the problem and the promise:

> Liberal Religious Youth is the only youth organization funded by the UUA, yet its programs and structure are having an effect in only about eleven of our twenty-three districts. Most of our districts have many new local youth programs that want programs and services on the regional and continental level, but past politics and performance make it difficult for them to organize under the LRY label. No one is more concerned about this than the leaders of LRY and the Board of the UUA. Together, they have agreed on a process which will bring together all of the LRY-affiliated and unaffiliated groups in the UUA into one, representative delegate body. This body will be asked to set a new direction, and possibly a new structure, for continental and regional youth programming in the UUA, a new direction and structure that everyone will support.

Although publicity material painted an optimistic picture of LRY and UUA co-operation, the existing LRY Executive Committee found the process deeply troubling. The youth assembly was designed to bring an end to LRY, an organization beloved by those who were a part of it. "We felt like we were preparing our own funeral," LRY Executive Committee member Lisa Feldstein remembers. "We were the targets of a lot of hostility, some of which was deserved but much of which was not. The idea that we were participating in the destruction of this thing we held as dear as life itself hung over us throughout the week." Feldstein describes LRY's overall feeling toward the UUA during this time as extremely negative: "We felt the UUA had unfairly forced us into this position, this process, and the UUA was hated."

However, Dave Williams, a member of LRY and the modera-

tor of Common Ground, believes that some of the misgivings held
by the members of LRY were misplaced:

> I think that most LRYers made a huge mistake, because I be-
> lieve that fundamentally, the process was trustworthy and
> open. And I believe that, because of LRY's leadership oppor-
> tunities and organizational history, LRYers, given a positive
> attitude and open-mindedness, could have come in and
> dominated the process, and done it fairly. Instead, LRY (and
> I include myself here) came with an attitude that nothing
> was broken, that not even the name should be changed, that
> any change would signal the end.

Despite the widely differing opinions of the conference attendees, the participants agreed to trust the process of the Common
Ground conference and abide by the collective outcome.

Choosing Representation

The planning for Common Ground began a year before the con-
ference. A "Youth Assembly Planning Committee," formed to de-
velop a process for the selection of delegates, consisted of Rev.
Anne Heller; UUA board member Charles Wyatt; UU Ministers'
Association representative Oren Peterson; youth members Kevin
Clark, Gretchen Jones, and Justin Alcorn; and staff member Rev.
Wayne Arnason.

The committee chose the name "Common Ground" for the
conference after Jim Scott's song of the same title (which some accounts have erroneously attributed to Paul Winter). Anne Heller
served as committee chair. "I had gotten to know Anne when she
was a member of SCOYP. She had been recruited for the committee because she was a nationally recognized regional Girl Scout
leader known to the UUA Moderator Sandra Caron, who also had
a strong history in Girl Scouts," Arnason recalls. "During the years
since SCOYP, Ann had completed her seminary training at Starr
King and was now an ordained UU minister. She was an extraor-

dinarily competent process person. She was a symbolic bridge to
the SCOYP Committee and the recommendations they had made
for a process such as we were trying to create. She was from a district that still had a strong LRY-style federation and local groups
functioning. She was someone I trusted."

Each district, through its board of trustees, was given authority to select youth and adult representatives to Common Ground.
This process met with controversy, as many LRY groups had little
or no connection to the UUA's district structure, let alone their
district boards. The Organizing Committee was up-front about
intentionally encouraging all youth to work with their districts in
order to become representatives. As the "Dozen Most Frequently
Asked Questions" flyer indicated, the committee wanted the districts "to feel like their delegates represented them" and trusted the
districts "to set up a selection process that would include all the
constituencies within the district that are concerned with youth
programming." Arnason spent a great deal of time on the road in
1980 and 1981, encouraging and attending district youth assemblies held for the purpose of selecting the delegation. He recalls
that most districts had a youth assembly, and "if they didn't have
one, they used as inclusive a process as they possibly could for
gathering a delegation together."

In contrast to LRY, which was entirely youth-led, Common
Ground aimed to design a new Unitarian Universalist youth organization co-led by youth and adults. With Common Ground
modeling the new structure, each district was invited to fill its delegate slots with a ratio of three youth to one adult. Overall, participants approved of the vision of youth and adult co-leadership,
and the three-to-one ratio in particular. However, concerns remained that adults would "take over" the proceedings instead of
participating in an advisory capacity. Feldstein recalls,

> The youth from some parts of the country where adults had
> run youth programming for a long time didn't really have
> the skill set to participate effectively, and their voices were
> not well represented. The Planning Committee was probably

a model of positive youth/adult interaction and respect, with leadership well shared. Common Ground-wide, I'd say we had belligerent and disrespectful youth and adults in equal measure, but some excellent shared leadership as well.

Process and Recommendations

The Planning Committee for Common Ground worked hard to structure this gathering of over 250 people to maximize participation and effectiveness. Following sessions of small working groups of about ten to fifteen people, each led by a trained facilitator, delegates assembled into one large group to integrate each small group's recommendations.

The business of the small groups and then of the delegates as a whole was framed around the following questions:

- Who will the new youth organization serve?
- What will its goals and purposes be?
- What form will this organization take?
- What will the process for change be?
- When and where will this new organization start?

Delegates Ben Ford and Laila Ibrahim and youth moderator Dave Williams all remember the first question as the most difficult. "It brought out very strong feelings remembers Ibrahim. "Was this organization just for teenagers?" In the end, Common Ground recommended an age range of twelve to twenty-two. That controversial recommendation would meet with further debate at Common Ground II and for years to come.

Williams feels,

It was a critical mistake to try to solve the problems of twelve-to-twenty-two-year-olds through the creation of a single organization. The issues faced by junior high, senior high, and post-high school Unitarian Universalists can't be easily lumped together, and many of the controversial 'behavior guidelines' discussed at Common Ground seemed to reflect the needs of the junior high-ers primarily. And the inclusion of post-high (nineteen to twenty-two) seems in retrospect like a bone that was thrown to those of us on the edge of getting kicked out. Wasn't it convenient for me to be on the [to-be-formed] YRUU Steering Committee at twenty, when at the same age I wouldn't have been eligible for anything in LRY?

Rev. Janne Eller-Issacs, speaking at a workshop on youth leadership at the 2003 General Assembly in Boston, echoed Williams's words:

"Who" was the first question addressed at Common Ground in 1981. And so all the resistance to creating a new organization and the grief over the loss of LRY got projected onto that first question. No one was willing to make hard fast boundaries as we responded to that question. So instead of asking "What is in the best interests of the youth movement, to make it a safe community for our youth?" we said, "How can we take care of all these grieving people?" We had nineteen- and twenty-year-olds standing up on the stage saying, "I'm losing everything."

Once the age range had been established, the "what" question followed. It was recommended that one brand-new Unitarian Universalist youth organization, dubbed the "Common Ground Baby," serve the whole age range. Local and district youth groups, both new and formerly associated with LRY, were to be clearly identified as Unitarian Universalist denominational groups, but individual youth would not need to be members of local congregations to participate. As in LRY, youth leadership would be a central component of the new organization, but there was a deliberate shift away from LRY model of "youth autonomy." For some, that shift was the most important resolution to emerge from the entire conference.

Goals and purposes were created for the still unnamed youth organization. They included "fostering spiritual depth, creating a peaceful community on earth and peace within us, and clarifying both individual and universal religious values as a part of our growth process," as well as to "encourage the flow of communication between youth and adults." The list of purposes went on to embrace diversity, individual freedom, and encouragement of individual responsibility. The new youth organization would also be charged with creating a network of youth groups and providing that network with the appropriate educational resources. These goals and purposes were consistent with what Arnason would call "the shift from LRY as a membership organization that was self-determining to YRUU, which was to be a service organization"

Common Ground also recommended that the UUA create a "section within the Department of Ministerial and Congregational Services" for the new youth organization, and that this "section," or department, be on par with other departments such as Social Responsibility and Religious Education. The section, they suggested, should be located at the UUA headquarters and staffed by both youth and adults. Finally, the Common Ground recommendations included the appointment of a youth representative from the new organization to the UUA Board of Trustees.

By the end of the conference, most delegates felt they had been lifted up by the process, holding their faith in a shared future and goodwill between youth and adults in front of them to light the way. Oren Peterson, an adult delegate serving on the Planning Committee, summed up his reflections in the *UU World* magazine:

> It is my assessment that we have traversed a chaotic era of social change and that Unitarian Universalists have been at the spearhead of such readjustment. As we have been the first to feel the effects of change, so may we be the first to chart a way to the future. Our Common Ground Youth Assembly may well be the precursor of what is to be. That is our vision, and we are determined to carry that vision home. You will hear from us, I promise you.

Anne Heller, the convener of the Planning Committee, says, "I felt exhausted and satisfied when I left. I felt we had accomplished the difficult task we set out to do."

For those who were still members of LRY and had effectively participated in the dissolution of the organization they loved, emotions were mixed. Feldstein says she felt "worn out and defeated." Within LRY, Common Ground participants would be ostracized and labeled as sell-outs by some fellow-members. For these delegates, the Common Ground process proved especially difficult. "One of the things that happened for me was the absolute pain at being singled out as the one who betrayed LRY," said former LRY member and Common Ground leader Rev. Julie-Ann Silberman-Bunn at a workshop on youth leadership at General Assembly in 2003.

Follow-up and Fallout

The delegates had hardly caught up on their sleep before post-Common Ground controversies arose. Skepticism about the UUA agenda arose when the UUA Board of Trustees didn't adopt the recommendation that the new youth organization become a new section of the UUA and have representation on the UUA board.

Arnason warned the Common Ground delegates that these proposals in particular might be in conflict with the UUA's overall plans. In a follow-up letter to Common Ground participants, he gently suggested that the delegates look over the reports from the Religious Education Futures Committee and the District Restructuring and Distributions of Resources (DR2): "The recommendation for a new youth section in the UUA, for example, is a suggestion that conflicts with the philosophy and direction of these other two reports. The UUA Board may be reduced in size by half under the DR2. How does this effect your thinking about Board representation for youth?" Despite Arnason's observations, many youth and adults who had participated in Common Ground feared that their doubts about the UUA's goodwill toward youth programming had been confirmed by its decision not to adopt these central recommendations.

According to President Pickett, the decision not to create a new section of the UUA for the youth "was partially a budgetary concern." In a letter to the president and Board of Trustees of the UUA, the Youth-Adult Committee and the Youth Programming Committee of the St. Lawrence District began, "We believe that you were sincere in your commitment to Common Ground and its outcome. However, recently your willingness to carry out the recommendations was put into severe doubt. We are referring specifically to the proposals by President Pickett to ignore the Continental Youth Assembly recommendations for a separate section for youth programming and a youth Trustee."

Similarly, Vonnie Hicks, an adult advisor and the Youth-Adult Committee co-chair from the Thomas Jefferson District, wrote that he was "appalled" to learn that the administration's recommendations to the UUA Board of Trustees involved rejecting Common Ground recommendations for a proposed youth trustee and a separate section within the UUA for the youth. Hicks' letter went on to say that, "What we are left with is a structure for a youth organization that would be adult-dominated, and a precedent of rule-making that confirms that perception."

Even more contentious than discussions of organizational hierarchy and structure was the question of sexual behavior rules, and their interpretations, at future UUA-sponsored youth events.

Standards of Behavior

The broad diversity of opinions about appropriate rules for sexual behavior at youth conferences became apparent at the staff-training weekend, and was a focal point of conflicting opinions throughout Common Ground. The Planning Committee had decided in advance on an official rule that "overt sexual behavior is strictly forbidden." In addition to this overarching rule, each delegation to Common Ground brought its own district's rules and norms around sexual behavior and co-ed sleeping at conferences.

Correspondingly, according to Common Ground's "Report of the 1981 UUA Youth Assembly Planning Committee to the UUA Board of Trustees," district delegations each had "the responsibility for enforcing their own standards on room assignments." Some district delegations permitted co-ed sleeping arrangements and some did not, and opinions were strong as to what was right and appropriate.

Members of some delegations complained and challenged the rules. A special, all-delegate meeting was held to air out the various opinions on the topic. Lisa Feldstein says, "Dealing with questions about whether it was appropriate for teens to have sex— married folks, straight, queer, etc.—and what 'overt' meant, was all-consuming and exhausting."

The Planning Committee took the complaints and debate under advisement but decided to let the wording of the original "no overt sex" rule stand. The Common Ground report excerpted the Planning Committee's statement as follows:

> The prohibition of "overt sexual behavior" as specified in the rules means "patently sexual, as contrasted with affectionate interchanges in public" . . . .
>
> Though we cherish our individual freedoms, privacies, and intimacies, we ask for temperance in all our doings in order to further the community.

The report went on to comment about the changing social norms around sexual behavior in the larger Unitarian Universalist and societal context:

> It is the belief of the Planning Committee that the issue around sexual behavior at Common Ground was a symptom of a larger dis/ease. Because we are a denomination that prizes the worth of the individual, we tolerate a broad spectrum of values among us. Consequently, our young people receive mixed and often conflicting messages from UU adults, particularly with regard to sexual behavior. We cannot expect consistent behavior from young adults if we do not

give them consistent expectations around that behavior. It is unlikely that much will change until UU adults come to a consensus about these issues among themselves.

Although the Planning Committee comments may seem both reasonable and accurate in hindsight, they did not prevent several participants, particularly the Unitarian Universalist Ministers' Association (UUMA) representative, Rev. John Robinson, from bringing complaints about the rules at Common Ground into a wider venue. As a result, Arnason spent a considerable part of his next year responding to various meetings and correspondence on this issue.

Robinson sent a proposal to the UUA board and to the other UUMA district chapter presidents to boycott all future continental youth events until the UUA adopted and enforced a strict "no sex" policy. Given that this adult-imposed recommendation came in conflict with the philosophy of youth/adult co-leadership, Arnason and the interim Continental Youth-Adult Committee prevailed upon President Pickett to reject Robinson's proposal and allow the fledgling committee to recommend a policy to the UUA Board of Trustees. Pickett supported the Continental Youth-Adult Committee, and the UUA Board of Trustees adopted its recommendation for a continental UU youth behavioral policy in January 1982. The policy prohibited alcohol and illegal drugs and forbade youth under the age of eighteen from indulging in sexual intercourse or patently sexual behavior or staying in co-ed housing at any youth events sponsored or financed by the UUA.

Various districts and congregations responded to the reports and rumors, mainly by publishing their own written statements. For example, the Board of Directors of the Central Midwest District states, "Whereas one of the prime reasons for UUA societies withdrawing from youth conferences and youth programs has been the lack of consistent rules of behavior and irregular enforcement of such rules . . . . the Central Midwest District goes on record as giving its support to only such high school-age conferences where there are clear rules of behavior prohibiting sex."

Rev. Frank Schulman, minister at Emerson Unitarian Church in Houston, Texas, and father of Common Ground delegate Andrew Schulman, also wrote to express his disapproval of what he characterized as tolerance of teen sex at conferences: "I speak only for Emerson Church in this matter, but we do not permit any conferences with coeducational living quarters . . . . I realize that this is not a new problem. It is one which has been around for a long time but it must be met with some firmness."

However, some districts, such as the Pacific Central District, considered the ambiguous nature of the rules to be in line with Unitarian Universalist values. They passed a resolution stating that they "affirm the principle and tradition of responsible freedom of conscience and choice in all matters of intimate personal relations, including sexual affection."

Some participants simply felt that the term "overt sex" was unclear and that the rules had not been explained clearly at the start of Common Ground. A report by the delegation from the Southwest District stated that the delegation "would like to reiterate the necessity for the use of clearly-defined terms in any rules statements that are placed in effect at any youth gathering. This will serve to make the rules easier both to follow and enforce. It also lessens the possibility of misunderstanding. By avoiding oblique terms, one also rules out the necessity for too much time-consuming clarification." Schulman echoed this concern in his letter, indicating that his son Andrew had been "irritated with the discussion because of the time it took from the main discussions."

The variety of district and local responses to the issue underscores the Common Ground Planning Committee's assessment that the wide variance in understanding about the rules governing "overt sex" and co-ed sleeping arrangements simply reflected confusion within the society at-large about the recent "sexual revolution"—combined with a disparity among UUs regarding how, or whether, rules should limit an individual's right to choose his or her own path.

Common Ground II

The goals for the 1982 Common Ground II conference were to approve a set of bylaws and to come up with a name for the "Common Ground Baby." Held from June 28 to July 3, Common Ground II immediately followed the UUA General Assembly at Bowdoin College in Brunswick, Maine.

As with the 1981 gathering, districts were charged with appointing their own delegations. About half of the appointed participants had attended the first Common Ground. At this highly structured follow-up conference, the first order of business was adopting official rules of procedure. In addition to business meetings, however, the conference offered a number of workshops, including:

- Games, Improvs, and Plays for Local Groups
- How to Make Rap Groups and Discussion Work in Your Local
- Youth Sunday Formulas that Work
- How to Survive Your Parents
- Political Action Issues for Your Local or District
- Dreamwork
- Nuclear Freeze Organizing
- Ministry to Young Adults
- District Youth-Adult Committee Organization and Ideas
- How to Get Things Done in the UUA (led by President Pickett)

Reflecting the hot topics of the day, these workshops demonstrated that the new youth organization had already begun to fulfill its mandate to provide resources and training for healthy local and district youth groups.

Common Ground II was Hank Peirce's first experience with Unitarian Universalist youth organizations at the continental level. Coming straight from Star Island's annual LRY week, he served as a youth delegate to Common Ground II from the Ballou-Channing District. Peirce remembers a lot of apprehension in the air, especially from the "older, hippie advisors who had been involved in LRY" and had come to Common Ground II with the express purpose of "aborting" the Common Ground Baby. In fact, Peirce reports that almost as soon as he arrived at the conference, Rufus Kaufman, an adult advisor from New York, called him into a meeting to strategize about how to stop the new Unitarian Universalist youth organization from coming into being and replacing LRY. Similarly, David Levine recalls that there were "rumors that the whole thing had been staged and that we had no real say in what was happening." Despite such efforts, the majority of conferees were clearly in favor of firming up and building upon the recommendations from the previous summer.

The business meeting entailed carefully reviewing each of the recommendations from the first Common Ground to decide how to implement them into the new organization's bylaws, a draft of which had been created in advance by the Continental Youth-Adult Committee. Despite another long, drawn out discussion, Common Ground II maintained support for the twelve- to twenty-two age range. The delegates also decided upon the composition of the new youth organization's governing body, "Youth Council," which was to have representatives from each district, along with a selection of other youth and adult representatives at-large. A Steering Committee was formed to meet several times during the year as the executive body of Youth Council. After creating the structure, the delegates elected an interim Youth Council and Steering Committee. The Interim Steering Committee consisted of David Williams, Laila Ibrahim, Dawn Johnson, David Levine, Mark Halsted, Vonnie Hicks, Lori Pederson (UUA Board of Trustees representative), and Nada Velimirovic (representing the Religious Education Advisory Committee).

One of the most interesting tasks of Common Ground II was naming the new organization. A suggestion box remained in place throughout the conference, with the final decision on the name pushed to the end of the agenda. Yet when the suggestions were pulled out of the box and discussed, no consensus or momentum formed around any of the ideas. The final list of potential names was:

- Free Religious Youth—70 votes
- Unitarian Universalist Youth—70 votes
- Young Religious Liberals—67 votes
- Liberal Religious Youth—61 votes
- Unitarian Universalist Youth Fellowship—61 votes

Despite the lack of a clear winner, the group plodded forward, whittled the list down, and finally voted for the name "Young Unitarian Universalist Fellowship," which allowed for the acronym, "YUUF Group." No sooner was it adopted, however, then one youth delegate declared the term "fellowship" to be sexist and, therefore, inappropriate.

Hank Peirce remembers that Rev. Bruce Southworth said to him the day before the name debate, "Hey, you've got a big mouth, come here. I've got to leave a day early, but if they still haven't got a name by tomorrow, I've got one—Young Religious Unitarian Universalists, or YRUU for short. You can tell them I said that." Peirce chose the moment after "YUUF Group" had been rejected to bring Southworth's idea to the floor. Levine recalls, "It was in the middle of the night on one of the last days, and we were all exhausted. The first reaction was 'That's dumb.' But over the next few minutes, the idea kind of grew on everyone until we were all really excited about it." The motion passed easily.

Play was considered an important part of work at Common Ground, and the youth developed many games and traditions that were as much a part of Common Ground II as they were of most youth conferences at the time. In the most popular game, "Wink," players raced on their hands and knees across a circle to be the first to tag the player who was "it." On the last night of Common Ground II, a huge game of Wink sent six people to the hospital. Injuries included a sprained wrist, a broken nose, a dislocated shoulder, and various scrapes and bumps. "There was so much energy going on that people didn't realize that other people had hurt themselves," one of the Wink casualties recalls.

Common Ground II was a significant conference for a number of reasons. In addition to shaping the Common Ground Baby into YRUU, it served as a model process for shared leadership between youth and adults. As youth delegate Andrea Dawson's feedback form indicated,

> There was a wonderful sense of shared commitment and of community. I think most people took home a great sense of accomplishment and a feeling of owning of, and commitment to, the group's decisions. This is about the best thing that could have come out of this conference. I don't really think the actual decisions (which varied very little from the Youth-Adult Committee's proposals) was as important as the (wince) process (forgive the word, please).

Another delegate wrote, "Never before have I gone from not knowing, to loving, so many people in so little time." Youth delegate David Levine wrote of feeling "Elated, drained, uplifted, very sad. I remember not wanting to leave but having to, because there was barely enough time to get to the airport in order to catch my plane. I think we had to drive to Boston or somewhere pretty far away. I was flying People's Express and I arrived at the airport just as the flight was scheduled to leave. The people at the ticket counter called the gate and they held the airplane, which had already started to taxi away from the gate (those days are long gone), and rolled one of those stairs up to it so I could board. I had to run through the airport with all of my luggage. I think I slept for the whole flight and about 18 hours after I got home. But I remember wishing that it would never end. That life would always be like it was at Common Ground."

The LRY Board of Directors held its last meeting at the end of Common Ground II. It moved to transfer what remained of its assets and any future gifts or bequests to the UUA for the benefit of youth programs. LRY also voted to cease operations at midnight on December 31, 1982. Accordingly, YRUU's birth certificate is dated January 1, 1983.

⌒℘↝

There was no youth group at my church per se; in fact, there were very few people under age sixty, and on Sunday mornings I went to the services with the rest of the congregation, and got a great deal out of them. I discovered that there was such a thing as a UU youth movement when my family attended Southeast Winter Institute Miami (SWIM), an intergenerational camp held between Christmas and New Year's. My brother and I stayed with the youth in a two-room dorm—there were about twenty of us, I think, ranging in age from thirteen to twenty. The dorm space was divided into loud and quiet, and in the loud room it never stopped. All but a very few slept in there on a long row of mattresses on the floor with our belongings underfoot. The first night, we sat up telling jokes and laughing for hours. It was a blast. I formed lifelong friendships that week, connected with people who continue to be among my dearest friends. No one there was exactly like me, but it was the first time I'd been in a group of teenagers and felt that I came even close to fitting in.

Youth-adult relations at the camp were pretty strained. The night that we told jokes until past 3:00 am, one of the adults from the next dorm over burst in and screamed at us to shut up. Our youth advisors were laid back and kind, but there seemed to be a history of the youth being "wild" and the adults doing their own thing. There were no intentional intergenerational events. The adults held a dance party every night to which no one under the legal drinking age (I think it was still nineteen then) was admitted, so plotting to sneak in and spy on them was a major activity. We hung around, visited the nearby bakery for cinnamon rolls and milk shakes, explored the woods without always the best of intentions, listened to records, and watched movies. I remember getting all dressed up for New Year's Eve and then falling asleep just after midnight in front of Monty Python's The Holy Grail.

At the end of the week, on New Year's Day, we cleaned and packed and said our goodbyes. We hugged and cried and passed around our mug books for signing. There was one girl a little older than me who wrote in my mine, "LRY lives!" I had no idea what that *meant, but my friend Mark Harris took me aside and told me that there were regular weekend conferences for youth and that he'd make sure to let me know about the next one, which was soon, in February. He had been involved in Common Ground, another term I was hearing but not connecting to anything, and he told me that things had changed, but that "It's not over."*

My parents took a leap of faith and allowed my brother and me —ages fifteen and fourteen, respectively—to take the bus on our own to the February, 1983, youth conference held in Clearwater, about a four hour drive from our home. It was the first YRUU event in Florida. When we arrived in the afternoon, there were very few people there, and no one we knew from SWIM. I felt like going back home. Mark was coming in on the bus from Miami, and would not arrive until 7:00 am the next day. I decided to stay up all night waiting for him. I can't even explain what a big deal this was for me, at fourteen, to be able to stay up all night. It was huge. Again, we hung out, listened to records, told jokes, and painstakingly created mailbags to be hung on the wall for incoming messages. A girl I remembered from SWIM arrived and I relaxed a little, but not much. Orientation was around midnight, and was kind of the breaking point for me. There were no games or introductions, and when someone said, "We all love each other here," all I could think was, "Love me? You don't even know my name." But everyone else did seem to know each other, and I felt painfully excluded. There was a lot of talk at orientation about old rules and new rules, LRY vs. YRUU, Common Ground, and a whole shared history that I wasn't part of and didn't understand. As soon as it was over, I found a place to be by myself and cried, And then remembered my determination to stay awake. I had a mission! I went back into the main room and hung around by the record player for the rest of the night. I remember that some of the others who were staying up made coffee, and I thought, how strange! To me, coffee was something my grandparents drank. I didn't need any kind of stimulant to keep me up.

Coleen Murphy
Fort Myers, Florida

The First Unitarian Society of Albuquerque was decidedly humanist, as you can tell by the name "Society." In Sunday School, a hippie lady sat cross-legged on the table playing guitar...and that's about all I remember of the early days, except for one more thing. General Assembly was in Albuquerque that year, and I marched in a demonstration with Bill Schulz, who I think was the director of social justice at the UUA at the time.

The middle school program prepared us for eighth grade with the About Your Sexuality *curriculum. We were certainly curious, but we were stunned by the film strips—it's like you're there, and I'd never been there. Our most important questions in life were answered, larger-than-life, on the projection screen. Those who went on to careers in sexuality education say that AYS was critical to their self-survival.*

Our best attempt at a name for the group was La Amikoj ("The Friends" in Esperanto, an artificial language that never quite got off the ground). But we usually called it Youth Group. The room was cozy for twelve youth in bean-bag chairs designed to be shared. Our meetings involved hang-out sessions with a lot of talk about what we were going to do. The advisor, a nice guy who really tried, had high hopes of programming something for us. We tried a few of the modules in Life Issues for Teenagers *on retreats, but the seriousness of the topics was beyond most of us, save for a few private-schoolers who had not taken AYS and did not know that there was more to life than thinking.*

The highlights of the early years in youth group were midnight movies, overnights, and hot-tubbing. We attended the church folk dance group sometimes, dancing the Hora and singing, "Maya, maya missed a soul," which we were sure was an ancient song about a Mayan goddess. I later learned the actual words are "Mayim, b'sasson," from an Israeli folk dance.

The youth group was all about us, and we came to know ourselves as free individuals. The concept of interdependence had not yet sunk in. But we did begin to get the idea of youth-adult cooperation. Older members of our group had attended Common Ground and had returned to tell us all about the new and improved youth movement called YRUU. We had no reservations about adopting the new name, since there were only one or two left from the old world, the LRY days.

Once the UUA sent a team from the Youth Office to present a leadership development conference. Mara Schoeny and Cappy Young had something to say about the components of youth programs, but all I remember was their smiles. Meeting celebrities from Boston was enough to motivate us to take up the cause; and if I remember correctly, it was to "organize."

In addition to adopting the cause, we became involved in every-con-under-the-sun-con, otherwise known as district youth conferences. We made up any excuse to hold a conference or attend one. We traveled great distances for weekend events, just to hang out with UUs in other states. Everything was "something"-con, named with forced puns and clever innuendos. Organizers made an effort to direct our desires toward social justice, and I think it stuck with many people. But I was content with back rubs and bubble-blowing. Ultimately, the communal experience was about consensus. We became an army of consensus builders for the rest of our lives.

A favorite game at conferences was "Amoeba," and I think it is an excellent symbol for UU youth. The game involves a small group of three or four youth interlocked in a group hug while their pseudopodia drags them across the floor. It chants "amoeba, amoeba," feeding on anything in its path, bringing others into the single cell until there is no one left but the Borg civilization that has assimilated all. It was our version of the one-world idea you find in the UUA Purposes and Principles—a kind of universal and homogeneous society, but on a microscopic level.

We always talked about the otherworldliness of youth group, the sense of community—which, for us, meant a feeling of acceptance by others. Ask anyone who was involved in youth conferences and they will remark on the intensity of the experience. We were free from all social conventions and labels. It was an experience of revolutionary freedom that would haunt me for the rest of my life. Today, I find it hard to imagine how we faced that abyss, but we were young and blissfully immortal.

Jason Happel
Albuquerque, New Mexico

Starting Over

YOUTH GROUP "generations" only last for four or five years, about the length of time it takes to go through high school. LRY soon became ancient history to the first generation of YRUUers, who dedicated themselves to getting YRUU up and running. They needed to put new institutional structures into practice and work out their kinks. The UUA Youth Office, Youth Council, and the Steering Committee called the vision and energy of a new set of Unitarian Universalist youth leaders into service. They focused on the annual conference ("Con-Con"), and the creation of much-needed programs, events, training, and other resources for local, district, and continental youth activities.

The Youth Office

In 1983, at the recommendation of Common Ground, the UUA established the Youth Office, which occupied a unique position within the association. As a part of the Department of Religious Education, it worked under, and received funding from, the UUA's departmental structure. However, in addition to the UUA, the staff of the Youth Office also reported to the YRUU Youth Council and Steering Committee.

The Youth Office began operations with three full-time staff —two youth programs specialists (renamed "YRUU programs

specialists" in 1990), who each worked for one year, and one ongoing youth programs director who was an adult. The youth programs
specialists had overlapping terms to allow continuity—one from
September to August, the other from January to December. A youth
programs specialist (YPS) had to be twenty-two or younger at the
start of his or her term. The YRUU Steering Committee received applications, conducted interviews, and selected a final candidate,
who was then approved by the UUA administration. The administration hired the youth programs director, who not only worked
with YRUU but was a member of the Department of Education
staff and responsible for curriculum development. In 1983, the first
curriculum in twenty-five years, *Life Issues for Teenagers*, was published. In 1984, Wayne Arnason stepped down from the youth director position and was succeeded by Rev. Ellen Brandenburg.

In its early years, youth who had attended or held leadership
positions at one or both Common Ground conferences held
most of YRUU's youth programs specialist positions. Julie-Ann
Silberman, David Levine, Colin Bird, Laila Ibrahim, Caprice
Young, Mara Lyn Schoeny, Erik Kaminetzky, Kathryn Deal, and
Scott Keeler were all keen to work in the Youth Office to pass their
vision and leadership onto the next generation. The Youth Office
modeled the kind of youth and adult collaborative leadership that
it encouraged in district and local youth groups.

Caprice Young describes her work in the Youth Office during
those early years of YRUU as energizing: "We were growing leaders
of all ages wherever we could find them." Julie Ann Silberman-Bunn
remembers that the youth staff had to live down LRY's "sex, drugs,
and rock 'n' roll" reputation to be taken seriously as colleagues.

> It was very interesting to be among the first in the Youth
> Office. I remember the staff from the Religious Education de-
> partment telling me after several months that they had been
> really worried and upset that we would be coming to work in
> their midst, but that we were far, far easier to get along with
> than they had feared we would be. They seemed to have some
> idea that we would have wild parties in the office with people

dropping by constantly and were very impressed to see us working and meeting with people instead of partying.

David Levine remembers that in the first years of the new UUA Youth Office, "There was still the 'awww, isn't that cute' factor working, meaning that we weren't really treated as regular staff but as some kind of amazing phenomenon, like when a baby takes its first steps or something."

In a 1988 interview about the Youth Office staff, Wayne Arnason expressed surprise that most of the youth programs specialists were between the ages of twenty and twenty-two as he had originally envisioned the youth staff positions as internships to be filled by high school-aged students. Such students would have brought enthusiasm and elbow grease, exercising those attributes under the adult youth programs director's supervision.

Arnason's vision for the YPS's was never realized. Youth programs specialists rejected the term *intern* from the beginning. And although no minimum age requirement is listed, no youth programs specialist has ever taken a year off of high school in order to take the job. The two youth programs specialists' positions were originally unsalaried; the youth who filled them received minimal stipends, designed to cover housing and living expenses. As Caprice Young (YPS from 1985-1986) recollects, it was a meager living. "We lived on the fifth floor of a walk-up on Cortez Street, by the Turnpike. I don't think that fewer than six people slept in that two-bedroom apartment on any night. All the youth knew we had an open-door policy and they used it pretty liberally. When we'd run out of food, we'd just go eat with the Moonies or the Krishnas."

By 1987, YRUU had lobbied successfully to turn the stipends into small salaries, including health care benefits. Survival in Boston depended on the fact that youth programs specialists continued to rotate in and out of the relatively inexpensive apartment on Cortez Street until 1989. The apartment, nicknamed "Scenic Overlook" for its fantastic view of the Massachusetts Turnpike, was anchored by a third, non-youth staff young adult named Bob King. Jason Happel (YPS from 1988 to 1989) remembers working and living with Leia Durland, Anne Sontheimer, and King at Scenic Overlook: "Leia made me carry her laundry to the laundromat. And I think I inherited the futon with a long and smelly youth staff history . . . something about bunnies or kittens, I don't know." When King and Sontheimer fell in love and decided to move out into a place of their own, the lease for Scenic Overlook was finally surrendered. To reflect the increase in the cost of living, YPS salaries jumped to approximately $14,000 per year in 1989 and then to about $16,000 a couple of years later as the UUA realized it needed to pay enough to allow safe accommodation in Boston.

As of 2004, forty-six youth/YRUU program specialists have each taken a year out of their lives to move to Boston and serve terms as YRUU leaders and administrators. Overall, the group has consisted of experienced Unitarian Universalists, many of whom have remained involved and committed to the faith. During these years:

- Five youth programs specialists have been ordained as Unitarian Universalist ministers or are currently studying for the ministry.
- Four have been elected to serve terms on standing committees of the UUA, including the General Assembly Planning Committee and the Ministerial Fellowship Committee.
- Four have gone on to other full-time work at the UUA, including positions at Beacon Press, the Washington Office for Advocacy, the Development Department, and the Religious Education Department.
- One is a director of religious education.
- Three are attorneys or in law school.
- One has been elected to public office as one of the board members of the Los Angeles Unified School District.
- Only two youth programs specialists have been fired.
- One person quit mid-term because she came to realize that she wasn't a Unitarian Universalist at heart.
- One person was unable to finish her term because she was arrested and imprisoned for civil disobedience at the Western Hemisphere Institute for Security Cooperation

(formerly the School of the Americas).
* One person has served two terms in the youth office.

Working and living relationships between the youth programs specialists often developed in very close quarters, resulting in fiery relationships of both the painful and the joyful kind. This intimate working relationship resulted in one marriage between two youth program specialists. Jennifer Martin and Sean Ramsey, who had worked together in the early 1990s, married after both had completed their terms.

Early Directions

Throughout the first years of YRUU, the youth programs specialists and the youth programs director shared the goal of creating new resources for Unitarian Universalist youth programs at the local, district, and continental levels. Four key handbooks were written over the next fifteen years: *The Local Youth Group Handbook*; *How to Be a Con-Artist: Youth Conference Planning Handbook*; *YACs to SACs: A Guide to District Programming*; and *The Youth Advisors' Handbook*. All four books had multiple authors and took several years and staff turnovers to complete. They compiled the most successful ideas, workshops, programs, and advice from YRUU groups from across the country.

In addition to these resources, a vision for the continual training of new youth and adult leaders was created during these early years. The first Continental Youth/Adult Leadership Development Conference took place in Dallas in 1986. Each district was invited to send one youth (aged sixteen or younger) and one adult for training to lead a newly developed weekend workshop about leadership styles and youth group development. Each youth/adult team was then required to return to its district and lead at least three weekend workshops for youth and their adult advisors over the next two years. The goal was to repeat a continental training of trainers every three years, to ensure that youth and adult leadership training remained continually available to local and district groups.

The success of this system of training trainers varied, based on the structure and health of each UUA district as well as its support for youth programming. In general, districts with active, well-established structures and boards had strong Youth-Adult Committees and took advantage of the resources and training offered, while districts with weak structures or little overall support for youth programs did not.

YRUU needed new systems of communication with Unitarian Universalist youth, as well as with local youth groups and adult advisors. The newspaper, *Synapse*, was created by and for YRUU members across North America. Edited by the youth programs specialists, it included information about upcoming YRUU events, artwork, creative writing, and articles about YRUU, social justice issues, and Unitarian Universalism in general. Youth programs specialist David Levine came up with the name:

> It was in the first year of YRUU at one of the Steering Committee meetings. I was at UC studying biochemistry and I had just done a paper on the neurotransmitter, acetylcholine. When I suggested it, everyone thought I was crazy . . . until I explained that the synapse is the point at which energy and information were exchanged . . . and the rest was history.

A newsletter, *Spider*, was created to keep Youth Council representatives informed, motivated, and on-task between annual meetings. *Spider* was retired in 1998, and due to budget cuts, the UUA decided to publish *Synapse* exclusively online on the YRUU web site in 2002. Happily, it returned as a print publication in November 2003.

An early goal of the UUA Youth Office and YRUU was to penetrate the UUA's administrative structure with as many youth as possible. Although they found no broad support for a youth position on the UUA Board of Trustees, youth could be nominated or elected to an existing position on a standing committee of the association.

One requirement for nomination to a UUA committee, however, is membership in a local congregation. Consequently, YRUU started a movement to encourage local congregations to lower their age of membership to twelve and to promote youth positions on their local boards. In 1985, Youth Programs Specialist Caprice Young remembers one of the biggest successes of her term as seeing "a bunch of youth elected or appointed to UUA board committees." The youth themselves had a role to play in these elections: "We had a real voice at General Assembly [1985] because we taught all the youth delegates Roberts Rules of Order at the start of GA."

Youth Council 1986 formalized the staff and organization structure for the annual, weeklong continental conference of YRUU, or "Con-Con." Surprisingly, the structure remains largely the same today, including such treasured traditions as the dance, auction, coffee house, morning workshops, the game Wink, and the "All-Day Super Special Surprise Activity." YRUU even carried some traditions forward from LRY that have made an impact in the wider Unitarian Universalist community. One such tradition is "touch groups," a form of small group ministry used to create meaningful community within a larger group. The small group ministry movement, now growing in popularity among Unitarian Universalist congregations, evolved in large part from the small-group traditions, or "touch groups," of YRUU and LRY.

Ben Ford remembers a tradition he began with others during the 1984 Con-Con at The Mountain, a Unitarian Universalist camp and conference center in North Carolina.

> At the auction, I bought a clove cigarette, advertised as the last one on the premises, for $15. I was in the back of the room, and thought I was bidding on a T-shirt—I wasn't even a smoker. But I pretended I had done it intentionally, and got Wayne Arnason to sign it (he wrote "Smoke it in good health" on it). It lived in a case in the YRUU office and came back to Con-Cons for several years. Rumor has it that someone smoked it in about 1988.

Throughout all of this institutional growth, YRUU continued in the tradition of deep social-justice commitment that had characterized Unitarian and Universalist youth organizations dating back to the turn of the twentieth century. With a 1991 Youth Council resolution, YRUU became one of the first Unitarian Universalist groups to actively work to create an inclusive space for gay, lesbian, and bisexual youth. As a continental organization, YRUU also worked to create a mechanism for local and district youth to network together on specific social-action issues. To that end, the 1990 and 1993 Youth Councils created the Social Action District Network as a way to use the Youth Office as a clearinghouse for information about grassroots social action activities. In addition, a continental social action coordinator was appointed to Youth Council.

YRUU has consistently sponsored workshops on current social-justice issues at Con-Con, as well as other social-action conferences including the UU United Nations Office Youth Conference and Continental Social Justice Conferences, held in conjunction with the UUA's office in Washington, D.C. More recently, making YRUU an anti-racist and anti-oppressive organization has taken top priority on the agenda. Beginning with a 1993 Youth Council resolution to incorporate racial justice and anti-oppression work into the structure of the organization, YRUU has set an example among Unitarian Universalist organizations of carrying out focused and challenging anti-racism efforts.

Age Range

The responsibility to meet the needs of junior, senior, and post-high youth never sat comfortably with YRUU. Although it embraced this age range in theory, it is fair to say that YRUU never had the staff or the resources to adequately serve the tremendously diverse needs of all three age groups. Several successions of Youth Council representatives throughout the 1980s and into the 1990s fought mightily over whether to lower the age range to fourteen to twenty, where it stands now. Youth Council 1984 had broken into small groups to discuss how best to meet the needs of these age ranges. Resolutions called for specific resources for these age ranges, but many of those resources were to be created by Youth Council volunteers who did not follow through with their commitments. The subject was still at the top of the agenda by the time of the 1987 Youth Council, which debated the issue at length and put forward resolutions to restrict the age range.

The UUA Board of Trustees' YRUU Five-Year Review Committee agreed that meeting the needs of the entire twelve to twenty-two age range under the existing structure was impractical. Its report stated, "YRUU is serving neither the junior-high nor the post-high age range effectively. The present twelve to twenty-two-year-old age range was a compromise to begin with, and discourages the kind of focused, age-appropriate programs that we feel best meet the needs of youth."

Junior high-school students were included in programs (such as Con-Con) that were functionally designed for older youth. The few early adolescents who attended these events were left to sink or swim there. Most simply didn't participate in YRUU at the continental level. The youngest participants at Youth Council and Con-Con were usually fourteen, and the Steering Committee frequently struggled to fill the junior high at-large position on Youth Council.

Following the recommendation of the YRUU Five-Year Review Committee, the 1989 Youth Council passed a resolution to raise the minimum age to fourteen, provided the following criteria were met.

- A junior high programs director position would be established within the UUA.
- The programs developed would focus on ages eleven to fourteen.
- Enjoyable programs for ages eleven to fourteen would be available in each district.
- Programs and support would be made available to develop leaders and advisors for this age range.
- Transition programs would be offered to support those coming into YRUU from groups for younger youth.

- The 1991 Youth Council would certify that all conditions had been met.

One concern in YRUU about raising the minimum age was that, although YRUU wasn't serving the junior-high age range well, it was better than no one serving it at all. The resolution's criteria attempted to address these fears and put pressure on the UUA to pick up the slack in junior-high programming. The 1991 and 1992 Youth Councils could not certify that the conditions had been met. Nevertheless, despite the continued absence of a junior high programs director on the UUA staff, the 1993 Youth Council approved the criteria for raising the minimum age, allowing it to take effect in January 1994.

Unfortunately, YRUU's concerns about the lack of programming for young teen-agers were justified. Models for religious education or groups serving junior high-aged youth are scarce. There are two notable exceptions. The first is the sexual education curriculum, *Our Whole Lives* (successor to the popular *About Your Sexuality*), often offered to twelve- and thirteen-year-olds. Second, many congregations have grown and developed coming of age programs, mostly on their own, for younger youth.

The upper age-range posed another vital question for YRUU. As former youth program specialist Eric Kaminetsky admitted, the limit of twenty-two had been created at Common Ground by youth who were in the post-high age range and didn't want to be "kicked out" of the new youth organization they had helped create. Addi-tionally, when YRUU was created, neither Unitarian Universalist congregations nor the UUA had provided any programmatic support for the post-high, college or young-adult age range.

In 1986, former members of LRY and people who had recently become too old for YRUU formed the grassroots organization, Continental UU Young Adult Network (C*UUYAN). One of the reasons Youth Council finally felt comfortable lowering the upper age-range to twenty was that, by 1989, the bare bones of C*UUYAN were in place, thus providing a place for "graduating" YRUU members to go. Youth changed YRUU's upper age limit to twenty, starting on January 1, 1992.

C*UUYAN

C*UUYAN offers two weeks of continental summer programming to Unitarian Universalists between the ages of eighteen and thirty-five. Opus, begun in 1986, served as C*UUYAN's first continental conference for young adults. In 1999, the business of running C*UUYAN was separated from Opus and moved to a distinct conference called Concentric. Since this structure mimicked YRUU's Youth Council and Con-Con, older YRUU members found it relatively easy to graduate from one organization to the next. Efforts were made in 1990, and again in 2000 and 2002, to hold the YRUU and C*UUYAN summer events near each other so older youth might move between the two events. The two groups experimented with program sharing in the form of a joint Coffee House at The Mountain Camp and Conference Center in 1990. The experiment flopped. Some old YRUU members came from Opus to Con-Con and put on their tried and true acts. These skits and songs had been YRUU traditions only a few years earlier; however, institutional memories of youth organizations are short, and the current pack of YRUU members didn't get the in jokes and were bored by the acts. It became clear to everyone in that moment that it was time for the older members of YRUU to move on.

Today, C*UUYAN is a thriving "sponsored organization" of the UUA, a status it shares with YRUU. Beginning with one half-time director of young adult ministries in 1989 (Rev. Terasa Cooley), the UUA Young Adult and Campus Ministry office now has a staff of four: a director, program associate, administrative assistant, and campus ministry director. When C*UUYAN began in 1986, the UUA was only aware of six Unitarian Universalist groups on college campuses in the United States and Canada. In 2003 those groups numbered over 125. The people who created C*UUYAN didn't wait for the greater denomination to recognize the pressing need for programs and resources for young adults;

they founded and built their own. Fortunately, the UUA recognized that C*UUYAN serves a core group of people looking for a spiritual home and made it a priority to fold the young adult programs into the budget and purview of the association.

Rules About Sex

The topic of rules around sexual behavior at YRUU continental events remained controversial and heated. Perhaps the staff at Common Ground had been prophetic in saying, "The issue around sexual behavior . . . was a symptom of a larger dis/ease."

Despite the debate that raged between the first and second Common Ground conferences more than two decades ago, the original rules, prohibiting "overt sex," "overtly sexual behavior," or "patently sexual behavior" by youth under the age of eighteen at UU conferences remain in place today. Given that such rules are, by their very nature, difficult to interpret and enforce with consistency, the 1986 Youth Council created a structure to deal with any rule infractions at YRUU's Con-Con. Just as the UUA cannot dictate practices to individual congregations, YRUU does not set the rules for local or district events. At the same time, Youth Council acted with the knowledge that continental-level activities often set a precedent for local and district activities.

The 1987 Con-Con report by Ellen Brandenburg, the second youth programs director, sums up her frustration about some of the inconsistent rules. Her comments characterize the ability of youth over the age of eighteen to elect to stay in co-ed cabins as unfair and against the community spirit that Con-Con is trying to create. YRUU maintains that intimate sexual behavior is detrimental to the overall conference community:

> We have tried to create an atmosphere where everyone feels acceptable and safe, and where there is no pressure to be coupled. The freedom that Con-Con allows people should not be taken advantage of for the purpose of sexual intimacy. Yet, by the laxity of our sleeping guidelines, and the lack of

conversation about the inappropriateness of sexual intimacy at Con-Con, we make it all too easy for it to occur. When couples emerge from the woods at 8:30 in the morning with sleeping bags over their shoulders, I feel that the spirit of what we would want Con-Con to stand for has been violated.

The different sleeping rules for those over and under the age of eighteen were finally changed in the late 1990s when Jennifer Devine was the youth programs director. Youth Council concluded that separate co-ed and same-sex housing rules were essentially heterosexist. Over the years, many YRUU members have argued that the best way to approach rule enforcement is to trust that conferees would uphold the covenant of "no overtly sexual" behavior, and that the mere existence of co-ed housing does not mean that this rule is automatically being broken. Instead of changing the differing rules for sleeping arrangements, conference organizers have created a more conscious and conscientious process for monitoring the spirit or "energy" of the conference as a whole.

Given the fact that it is time-consuming to work through the consequences of rule infractions on a case-by-case basis, a committee of youth and adults, called the "Energy Committee," was created to attend to these issues in the late 1980s. This committee functions separately from the main staff group for the conference, allowing the dean, workshop co-ordinator, and other staff to have time to run the programs and events.

Despite these accountability structures, some adult advisors remained concerned around the ambiguity of the "no overtly sexual behavior rule" into the 1990s. Earlier, however, some of this anxiety was ameliorated when the lower age range was raised to fourteen.

Reclaiming the LRY Endowment Fund

Graham Smith, a member of the YRUU Steering Committee from 1989 to 1990, was reading over the Common Ground II report when he noticed its references to fact that the the LRY endowment had been turned over the UUA for the benefit of youth programs.

At the time, YRUU was not receiving any specific income from such an endowment and there was no such income line item in YRUU's budget from the UUA.

Further investigation revealed that the money had indeed been turned over to the Unitarian Universalist Association upon the dissolution of LRY, but then simply added to the general endowment fund and forgotten.

The Steering Committee committed itself to reclaiming YRUU's right to the income from the LRY endowment. Under pressure from YRUU to account for the missing LRY endowment income, the UUA administration traced the history of the money's mismanagement and calculated its present value. David Provost, the UUA's treasurer at the time, attended the spring 1990 Steering Committee meeting to present various income investment and distribution options for the committee's consideration. Provost notes that the LRY endowment was not the only fund to have been misused by the UUA in this manner. He notes that, from the time of the merger between the Unitarians and Universalists in 1961 and continuing into the 1980s, the "UUA's financial records [had been] in disarray for years" and that "by the 1980s, the UUA was well in to the mode of robbing Peter to pay Paul. The UUA's expenses out-stripped its income. The then-CFO unilaterally utilized cash from wherever he could find it in order to cover the Association's expenses."

Although the endowment income was restored, the UUA did not initially distribute the money on top of the amount allocated to YRUU in the UUA's overall budget. Consequently, the correction failed to yield an immediate increase in available funds. The issue remained dormant until the report of the 1997 Youth Programs Review Committee, which recommended that

> the UUA Board of Trustees place the LRY endowment income, currently integrated into the UUA budget, under the direct control of YRUU with the understanding that that amount will be replaced in the youth program budget from General Fund monies; that the Steering Committee of

YRUU be the executors of the LRY endowment income at the will of the Youth Council.

The Review Committee believed that failure to give YRUU direct control of the endowment income contradicted the youth empowerment the UUA professed to support. It continued,

> We do not advocate leaving youth with sole control over their entire program budget, since the history of LRY illustrates that this amounts to an abdication of adult mentorship and responsibility and can therefore result in the deterioration of youth programming. But we do feel it is important for YRUU to have a source of income which the Youth Council and Steering Committee can apply at their own discretion to interests outside the normal maintenance of the organization.

The Youth Council of 1997 passed a resolution in support of this recommendation. The UUA Board of Trustees agreed, and the income from what had once been the LRY endowment is now budgeted and spent by the Youth Council.

The Youth Voice at General Assembly

The relationship of the Youth Caucus at the UUA's General Assembly to YRUU has never been formal or clear. The Youth Caucus pre-dates YRUU, having represented the interests of Unitarian Universalist youth since the 1969 General Assembly in Boston. It is a venue for both youth delegates and non-delegates to debate and strategize around the issues of the Assembly as a whole.

When created in 1983, the Youth Office (as part of the UUA) took over the organization and staffing of the GA Youth Caucus, and programming continued as in years past.

In the mid-1980s, a youth volunteer position of business manager was created, and the Youth Office organized and supervised separate youth housing for those youth who chose it. In 1989, about seventy youth stayed in the youth housing. Many attended without their parents but under the supervision of adult sponsors from their home districts or congregations.

Youth Caucuses since 1986 have become almost completely separate conferences at General Assembly. They are often larger continental youth conferences than Con-Cons.

In earlier years, Youth Caucuses focused on business coming before the plenary sessions at General Assembly. Youth Caucus participants were all taught the rules of procedure that governed plenary sessions in order to facilitate their participation. Youth Caucus reached consensus opinions about resolutions facing the Assembly and then selected a Youth Caucus member, who was also an official delegate from his or her congregation, to speak on behalf of the Caucus.

The popularity of Youth Caucus as a "youth conference" grew steadily until it exploded in 1996 in Indianapolis, Indiana. That year, with the whole General Assembly adopting a "Youth Focus," attendance in the Youth Caucus reached a high of 348. Former youth program specialist Sarah Gibb remembers that UUA President John Buehrens had come up with the idea of the Youth Focus at GA and pushed for it: "He originally wanted GA 1995 to be a Youth Focus, but was persuaded by the youth programs director, Jory Agate, and others, to delay until 1996." Since the decision to move the Youth Focus to 1996 had left an opening, GA 1995 had a young adult focus instead. Gibb served on the task forces that created special programming for both the young-adult and youth-focused GAs. The 1997 Youth Programs Review Committee concluded in its report, "Through workshops, worship services and presentations at the GA plenary, this event was highly successful in exposing over 3,000 UU adults to our unique philosophy of youth empowerment and promoting youth programming as a priority in our denomination."

Interest and participation in youth and young-adult programming at GA have continued to increase since then. The 2003 General Assembly in Boston saw another record high, with 750 youth participants. The large numbers are in part simply a function of demographics; youth of the late 1990s and early twenty-first century, children of the Baby Boomers, now make up the second largest generational group, behind only their parents. With so many participants, the Youth Caucus's strict focus on General Assembly plenary sessions has ceased to be practical or even possible.

YRUU as a Sponsored Organization

In 1998, the UUA Board of Trustees granted YRUU unique status as a "sponsored organization" of the association. This new status was meant to clarify YRUU's relationship to, and place within, the UUA. Although YRUU has its own organizational structure and leaders, its programs and staff are financially supported by the UUA. The Youth Office reports to two distinct bodies, the YRUU Youth Council and the UUA administration. From time to time, these two entities have conflicting priorities for the Youth Office, so it has been difficult to know to which "boss" the youth staff must answer.

The "sponsored organization" status was designed to reflect the Unitarian Universalist philosophy toward youth programs. Teenagers need and want to play a key role in the creation and determination of their own programs. The UUA supports that desire, as do districts and most congregations. However, the larger denomination realizes that it isn't appropriate to expect youth to raise their own operating funds or expect adults to abdicate all responsibility as advisors and mentors. YRUU's sponsorship by the UUA reflects this understanding. In effect, a covenant based on trust has been created between the youth and the UUA, with UUA financing YRUU but the youth, with adult participation, guiding their own organization.

This somewhat ambiguous status is perhaps both YRUU's greatest strength and its greatest weakness. Freed from the ups and downs of youth-only leadership and the burden of self-financing, YRUU is at liberty to focus on programming, resources, and networking, taking advantage of the administrative infrastructure of the greater association. Over the years, however, the fact that the youth staff is ultimately accountable to the UUA administration and not to the YRUU Youth Council or Steering Committee has created a number of points of tension.

By and large, the UUA has trusted the YRUU Steering Committee to recommend appropriate candidates for the youth programs specialist positions, while functionally, the Steering Committee and YRUU Youth Council have provided direction and focus for the work of the Youth Office. From time to time, however, incidents have arisen to remind YRUU of its status as a "sponsored organization."

In YRUU's early years, trust between the youth staff and the rest of the UUA was sometimes fragile, with youth programs specialists forced to lobby for the same rights enjoyed by the rest of the staff. Scott Keeler (YPS in 1987) remembers "fighting, and succeeding, for the trust of the administration for youth programs specialists to have access to their offices for times other than strictly normal working hours."

The parallel power structures of the UUA Board of Trustees and YRUU Youth Council may ultimately leave enough ambiguity over who is in charge to confuse both the youth and the adult advisors. Does the Youth Council have the authority to set the direction for youth programs, as its own bylaws suggest? Or does the UUA have the ultimate power, since the Youth Office staff is a part of the UUA as a whole, and the staff of the Youth Office does the majority of the work for YRUU?

Youth Representation on the UUA Board of Trustees

It had taken twenty years, but 2002 finally saw the fulfillment of Common Ground's recommendation to have a voting youth on the UUA Board of Trustees. YRUU, along with some of its adult allies, had begun slowly discussing the idea in the late 1990s. In 1998, Youth Council passed a resolution to "Create a YRUU Trustee At-Large on the UUA Board of Trustees." That resolution included a mandate for a representative from YRUU to attend all the 1999 and 2000 UUA Board of Trustee meetings, to demonstrate commitment and interest and to lobby for the change.

Two former Youth Council representatives, Elizabeth Capone-Newton and Abbey Tennis, attended the October 1999 Board of Trustees meeting to propose a youth trustee. They met with the religious education working group, where the idea encountered mixed support. Some Trustees supported the idea of a youth on the board in principle but felt that they couldn't allow one "interest group" to have a seat without opening the floodgates for all sorts of other identity-based groups to expect the same.

However, the idea of a youth trustee was slowly gaining momentum. Although the proposal had been rejected in past years, the Board of Trustees now included several former LRY members. Wayne Arnason, Larry Ladd, and moderator Denny Davidoff all spoke in favor of having a youth trustee. Their support, together with YRUU's lobbying, made the difference.

During this time, ongoing discussion addressed potential re-organization of the board as a whole. However, the UUA board decided not to wait until that conversation was finished before moving forward on the youth trustee question. The board felt that it could not favor YRUU above all other Unitarian Universalist identity groups by allowing the youth trustee to represent YRUU directly. Two Youth Observers were appointed as non-voting participants in January 1999 with the simple goal of bringing youth voices to the table. Abbey Tennis remembers being at the board meeting where she was appointed as one of the first two youth observers:

> Someone on the board made the formal proposal that two Youth Observers should sit at the table with equal say until the board either restructured or added a voting youth member. The Board voted "yes," and Billy Sinkford Jr. and I went up to sit with them—for the first time in history. Later that morning, [Board member] Gini Courter said something to me like "Abbey, you know what's sad? When you and Billy sat down at the table with us, you not only added two youth

voices, but you doubled the number of queer people and people of color at this table." At that point, the only other person of color on the Board was Norma Poinsett. We left the meeting feeling like we had made a difference, that change was in the air.

In June 2002 the General Assembly completed the bylaw change that put one voting youth trustee in place. The second youth observer position remained unchanged. As it does for the other board positions that are elected at General Assembly, the Nominating Committee nominates a candidate for the ballot.

Jacob Larsen, who served as the board's fourth youth observer, feels that expectations for the position should be the same as those for any member of the board.

> I hope they will continue the trend toward significant involvement in the Board—serving as Board-appointed liaisons to various committees and task forces. I hope some of the realistic, vision-centered governance that I have experienced, and been so inspired by, will filter through the youth and young adult communities. Also, simple dialogue—knowing "what's up" with your neighbor—is something that will help us build better, more thoughtful religious communities and benefit us all.

With the creation of the youth positions on the UUA's Board of Trustees, the denomination as a whole showed agreement with Jacob's desire to ensure that youth leaders are welcomed as partners in shaping the future of Unitarian Universalism.

☙

In my rural-suburban world, no one knew about Unitarianism and Universalism. In an intellectual and spiritual sense, I really didn't either as a youth. Going to church as a family was our weekly practice, however, and the West Hills Unitarian Fellowship was a home away from home from the 1970s to the early 1990s.

Our youth group at WHUUF (pronounced like 'woof') was the center of that home and we had a lot of pride, having been told we were the first to have a core group that met regularly. There were a solid ten of us, with another thirty on the mailing list. We were connected inter-generationally throughout our church, but unfamiliar with the life of other youth. This was in 1985.

I first realized that there was continental YRUU in 1989 when I began the first of two two-year terms on the Pacific Northwest District Youth-Adult Committee (YAC). YRUU, from a historical perspective, was still very new and a lot of mystery surrounded its predecessor, Liberal Religious Youth. Some of this mystery manifested itself through tense youth-adult relationships and interactions. As an outspoken and highly energetic youth organizer, I personally experienced a great deal of ageism and miscommunication (however unintentional) from adults in roles of stewardship.

Looking back, however, I have been personally transformed by the activities of YRUU and have had the privilege, these last few years in my UUA role, to observe the incredible leaps the community has taken and how YRUU is even more impressive than ever. One area is in anti-oppression, and most importantly, identity-positive community development. I believe this new identity-positive environment fosters a stronger spiritual community, allowing our youth to deeply explore the diverse people they are. From age, gender, and class to theology, relationships and money, today's youth look at these pieces of who we are.

As I was graduating in 1991, my life was gripped by the first American War in Iraq. I remember distinctly using my dad's old IBM XP to run conference registration in Lotus 1-2-3, phoning and writ-

ing fellow-YRUU folks, and losing touch after leaving YRUU. I will never forget days with other Unitarian Universalist youth at anti- war meetings and actions, with intense learning in a short time pe- riod and my first direct action experience.

We were horribly out of touch with local youth groups from a district YAC point-of-view. A reform of the YAC structure and elec- tions and the development of "youth group clusters" within our large geographic district were primary among our new initiatives. While I saw only the beginnings of these campaigns, they were eventually successful and had some small impact on the continental YRUU. It is hard to explain the groundswell of energy in YRUU from 1991 to 1996. For me it culminated in the famous Youth Focus GA in 1996. Another project originating in the Pacific Northwest District, which has now become a centerpiece at the UUA, is the Bridging Ceremony from youth to young adulthood.

As a Youth Council representative from 1991 to 1992 and YRUU Steering Committee member from 1992 to 1993, I became even more aware of the echelons of youth leadership. My sense of "climbing the social ladder" was intense and frustrating because I struggled with my local commitment as a continental leader.

At my last Con-Con, in 1993, it felt like I was leaving a summer camp community . . . I found intense relationships at conferences, a wonderful local youth group that was like family (the good and the bad), and some extraordinary opportunities to be in serious leader- ship roles. What I yearned for, and see slowly being provided today, was an awareness of the diversity of people within our community and the wholeness of people's selves. This growth of YRUU is impor- tant, and continues to place YRUU at the progressive and grassroots center of our Unitarian Universalist faith.

I still keep track of friends from my days in YRUU, and count several among my best friends. But YRUU has issues that need to be considered through consensus and infinite potential to consistently do justice with accountability and be welcoming and affirming. As generally the first and largest community our young adults have be- fore they start their journey to new life opportunities, such as chil-

dren, careers and making a home, YRUU flirts outrageously with the power of youth and the privilege of being a significant socially-conscious stakeholder in UUA and world politics.

Joseph Lyons
Portland, Oregon

Paths in the Jungle

COMMON THREADS have linked Unitarian, Universalist, and Unitarian Universalist youth organizations. Our faith teaches that each of us has the responsibility to find our own truth. Unitarian Universalism has always encouraged its youth to undergo that process for themselves. The Principles of the Unitarian Universalist Association also emphasize the value of democratic process, and all the youth organizations have used the democratic process to chart their own course into the future.

Many former participants who come back to Unitarian Universalist youth groups today find these same core values. One such person is former LRY Executive Committee member, and Common Ground moderator Dave Williams:

> Since 1984, I've had two experiences with YRUU; one on the local level and one on the district level. In both cases, I felt a huge sense of connection to what we created at Common Ground I and II, and in fact, to LRY. The issues the kids face were similar, and the opportunities for growth, change, and leadership were still there. The chance to be a freak and not pay a price was still there. In 1997, I attended a Pacific Northwest District youth conference in British Columbia, attended by 250 youth, that could have been mistaken for any LRY conference of my youth—with all that entails, both good and bad.

It is difficult to make predictions about the future of the Unitarian Universalist youth movement. It has remained rooted in local groups attached to Unitarian and Universalist congregations, and these local groups and district structures are stubborn organisms. Where youth groups fade, they are quickly revived once a new group of teenagers needs a youth program.

YRUU and all its ancestors—LRY, AUY, UYF, YPRU, and YPCU—have all been outgrowths of young people's need to share, grow, and expand their awareness and skills. The larger denomination's continued support of an essentially self-determining continental youth program has added a unique dimension to its participants' experience over the years. Structures, leadership styles, and relationships with advisors and staff have changed to suit the times and will continue to do so. Such changes have not, and need not in the future, threaten the integrity of the educational philosophy underlying our youth programs.

The reflections of Hugo Holleroth concerning the philosophy of religious education undergirding the 1970s curriculum series of the Unitarian Universalist Association are relevant to Unitarian Universalist youth programs and organizations, past and present. Holleroth asserts that we live in a world filled with power. He summarizes the objectives of Unitarian Universalist religious education as follows:

> The overall objective of Unitarian Universalist religious education is to help children have a vivid and compelling experience of the Unitarian Universalist religion to help them achieve an orientation to the world. More specific objectives include helping them:
>
> - become aware of and comprehend the multitude of powers within the self as well as those which impinge upon them from the environing world,
> - discover and become skilled in using the process which is the Unitarian Universalist religion, and,
> - use the process which is the Unitarian Universalist

religion for relating to and dealing with the ways they are affected by the world as intellectual, moral, sentient, aesthetic, and mortal beings.

Adolescence is one period in life when people become acutely aware of the powers that impinge upon them from within (such as their own sexuality), as well as the powers that impinge upon them from without (such as institutional restrictions). Adolescence is also a time when individuals can find within themselves, the personal power to actively respond to these powers.

Adam Auster, a member of the LRY Executive Committee in the 1970s, reflected on the Unitarian Universalist approach to youth programming at a workshop during the 2003 General Assembly in Boston. He spoke about LRY specifically, but reflected a philosophical understanding that all Unitarian, Universalist, and Unitarian Universalist youth organizations share:

> How do you teach democracy, critical thinking, freedom? How do you really empower? What method best serves those values? Rote memorization and reciting the catechism don't seem to cut it, yet neither does sink-or-swim. The Unitarian Universalist answer was to empower the young folks with their own organization, their own leadership, and their own budget. Influence them by dialogue and engagement. Resolve differences through good-faith negotiation, even if that is difficult. Commit to give, as well as take. It was unusual; it's moving, and very UU.

The youth movements have offered young people the opportunity to explore for themselves the dynamic between freedom and responsibility in personal and institutional life. Freedom and responsibility cannot be understood as abstractions, only grasped in living situations where real freedom and its consequential responsibility are present. This is the primary educational process at work within the chaos of local group meetings and district and continental conferences.

Another crucial educational process in our youth movement

is exposure to the problems of life in groups and institutions. The themes of personal liberty versus collective discipline, ideals versus institutional necessities, and individuality versus group identity have consistently been part of the young people's experience within our youth movement.

The only thing we can count on for the future is that Unitarian Universalist youth will continually reinvent the wheel. Youth advisors know the pattern well. This circularity has ranked among the most frustrating patterns for people involved in our youth movements over a long period of time. Similar problems, and similar solutions, occur and recur.

Yet new environments surround the old problems, and the solutions are never quite the same as those of last year. Reinventing the wheel is one of the purposes of a youth organization. There are no wisdom books or manuals to get people through adolescence into adulthood. It's like the image of the jungle in Gabriel Garcia Marquez' *One Hundred Years of Solitude*. One person hacks a path through the jungle, but it grows back as thickly as before as soon as the passage has been made. All that remains are stories of how the trail was made, there are no markers to show you where it lies.

APPENDIX 1

Acronyms

AUA	American Unitarian Association
AUY	American Unitarian Youth
C*UUYAN	Continental Unitarian Universalist Young Adult Network
COG	Community of Growth
CSA	Committee for Study and Action
DRE	Director of Religious Education
IARF	International Association for Religious Freedom
IRF	International Religious Fellowship
LRY	Liberal Religious Youth
MARC	Middle Atlantic Regional Committee
MICON	Midwest Regional Committee
NERC	New England Regional Committee
PNWD	Pacific Northwest District
SCOYP	Special Committee on Youth Programs
SELRY	South East Liberal Religious Youth

SFRL   Student Federation of Religious Liberals

SRL   Student Religious Liberals

UCA   Universalist Church of America

UGC   Universalist General Convention

UUA   Unitarian Universalist Association of Congregations

UUMA   Unitarian Universalist Ministers' Association

UYF   Universalist Youth Fellowship

WFDY   World Federation of Democratic Youth

YAC   Youth-Adult Committee

YPCU   Young People's Christian Union

YPRU   Young People's Religious Union

YPS   Youth Programs Specialist

YRUU   Young Religious Unitarian Universalists

APPENDIX 2
Youth Movement Presidents

YPRU

1896-1898	Thomas Van Ness
1898-1899	Roland W. Boynton
1899-1900	Walter Prichard Eaton
1900-1901	Roger S. Forbes
1901-1902	Percy A. Atherton
1901-1903	John Haynes Holmes
1903	Edward Marsh
1903-1904	Earl C. Davis
1904-1905	Carleton Ames Wheeler
1905-1906	Edgar S. Wiers
1906-1908	Harold G. Arnold
1908-1911	Henry G. Saunderson
1911-1913	Dudley H. Ferrell
1913-1916	Sanford Bates
1916-1918	Frederick M. Eliot
1918-1919	Carl B. Wetherell
1919-1921	Houghton Page
1921-1922	Chester Allen
1922-1924	Albert A. Pollard
1924-1926	Edward P. Furber
1926-1928	Charles S. Bolster
1928-1931	Frank B. Frederick

1931-1933	Dana McLean Greeley
1933-1935	Bradford E. Gale
1935-1938	John W. Brigham
1938-1939	Roland B. Greeley
1939-1941	Henry V. Atherton

YPCU

1889-1892	Lee E. Joslyn
1892-1894	Herbert Briggs
1894-1897	Elmer Felt
1897-1900	Harry M. Fowler
1900-1905	Louis Annin Ames
1905-1907	Frederick W. Perkins
1907-1910	Harry R. Childs
1910-1912	A. Ingham Bushnell
1912-1915	Stanley Manning
1915-1917	George A. Gay
1917-1918	Hal Kearns
1918-1919	Eleanor Bisbee
1919-1920	Samuel Cushing
1920-1921	Clifford Stetson
1921-1922	Charles Taylor
1922-1923	Ernest Jones
1923-1926	Ellsworth Reamon
1926-1929	Carl Olson
1929-1930	Dorothy Tilden Spoerl
1930-1932	Max A. Kapp
1932-1934	Stanley Rawson
1934-1936	Arthur Olson
1936-1939	Benjamin Hersey
1939-1941	Fenwick Leavitt

AUY

1941-1943	G. Richard Kuch
1943-1945	Arnold F. Westwood
1945-1947	Elizabeth Green
1947-1948	David B. Parke
1948-1949	Kurt Hanslowe
1949-1950	Charles W. Eddis
1950-1952	C. Leon Hopper
1952-1953	Eileen Layton
1953-1954	Clara Mayo

UYF

1941-1943	Dana Klotzle
1943-1945	Ann Postma
1945-1946	David Cole
1946-1948	Robert H. MacPherson
1948-1949	Carl Seaburg
1949-1951	Charles Collier
1951-1954	Rozelle Royall

LRY

1954-1955	Clara Mayo
1955-1957	Robert Johnson
1957-1958	Richard Teare
1958-1959	Spencer Lavan
1959-1961	Jerry Lewis
1961-1962	Mary Vann Wilkins
1962-1963	Maria Fleming
1963-1964	Charles A. Forrester
1964-1965	Frederick West
1965-1966	William G. Sinkford
1966-1967	Ruth Wahtera
1967-1968	Gregory H. Sweigert

1968-1969	Lawrence R. Ladd
1969-1970	Robert L. Isaacs (now Eller-Isaacs)
1970-1971	Lawrence Brown
1971-1972	Charles B. Rosene
1972-1973	Gale Pingel

In August 1973, the LRY board abolished hierarchical officer roles, including president. The LRY Executive Committee operated as a role-based executive collective, so all Executive Committee members after 1973 are listed below.

1973-1974	Adam Auster, Peter Nalven, Paula Rose, Matthew Easton
1974-1975	Lara Stahl, Bev Treumann, Steven Wilcox, David Knight
1975-1976	Carlotta Woolcock, Lynn Rubinstein, Jennifer Shaw, Richard Taeuber, Gary Decker
1976-1977	Emilie Blattman, Andrew Hanson, Paul Pigman, Doug Webb
1977-1978	Abbe Bjorklund, Susan Buis, Shelley Cantril, Barbara Dykes
1978-1979	Shelley Cantril, Katrinca Ford, Denise Lewis, Nada Velimirovic
1979-1980	Cheryl Markhoff, Laurel Prager, Dave Williams, Gretchen Jones
1980	Dave Williams, Gretchen Jones, Nina Martin, Julie Farman
1980-1981	Julie Farman, Nina Martin, Nan Warshaw, Amy Shapiro
1981	Nan Warshaw, Amy Shapiro, Kathryn Price, Lisa Feldstein
1981-1982	Lisa Feldstein, Becca Kovar, Paul Vail, Phil Rodgers

UUA/YRUU Youth Office Staff

UUA/YRUU Youth Programs Specialists

Julie-Ann Silberman (now Silberman-Bunn)	January–September 1983
Colin Bird	January–December 1983
Mara Lyn Schoeny	September 1983–August 1984
Eric Kaminetsky	January–December 1984
Laila Ibrahim	September 1984–August 1985
Caprice Young	January–December 1985
David Levine	September 1985–August 1986
Kathryn Deal	January–December 1986
Meg Wilson	September 1987–August 1988
Scott M. Keeler	January–December 1987
Andrew Moeller	September 1987–August 1988
Leia Durland (now Durland-Jones)	January–December 1988
Jason Happel	September 1988–August 1989
Anne Sontheimer (now King)	January–December 1989
Rebecca Scott	September 1989–August 1990
Adam Leite	June–December 1990
Parisa Parsa	September 1990–August 1991
Christine Murphy	January–December 1991
Julie Rising	September 1991–August 1992

Sean Ramsey	January–December 1992
Jennifer Martin	September 1992–August 1993
Serena Smallin	January–December 1993
Lorne Tyndale	September 1993–August 1994
Dan Ross	January 1994–February 1995
Sarah Gibb	September 1994–August 1995
Jenny Axel	January–April 1995
Rob Cavenaugh (now Keithan)	May–December 1995
Rachel Reed	September 1995–August 1996
Kathy Daneman	January–December 1996
David Taylor	September 1996–August 1997
Marc Loustau	January–December 1997
Alison Purcell	September 1997–August 1998
Sienna Baskin	January–December 1998
Austin Putman	September 1998–August 1999
Nathaniel Klein	January–December 1999
Duncan Metcalfe	September 1999–August 2000
Nathan Staples	January–December 2000
Abbey Tennis	September 2000–August 2001
Graham Baas	January–December 2001
Robin Scott Lea	June 2001–May 2002
Paula Nett	September 2001–August 2002 and April–June 2003
Wendell Seitz	January–August 2002
Megan Tideman	June 2002–May 2003
Tim Macpherson	September–Dec. 2002 (part-time)
Mimi LaValley	September 2002–March 2003 and August 2003
Bryan Beck	January–December 2003
Megan Selby	June 2003–May 2004
Jason Lydon	September 2003–August 2004
Betty Jeanne Rueters-Ward	June 2004–May 2005
Brian Kuzma	September 2004–August 2005

APPENDIX 4
UUA/YRUU Youth Program Directors

Rev. Wayne Arnason	1980–1984
Rev. Ellen Brandenberg	1985–1989
Rev. Meg Riley	1989–1992
Rev. Jory Agate	1992–1997
Jennifer Devine	1997–2002
Jesse Jaeger	2002–Present

APPENDIX 5
Presidents of IRF

1934-1938	Stewart Carter (Great Britain)
1938-1939	Jeffrey Campbell (USA)
1947-1948	G. Richard Kuch (USA)
1948-1949	Ludek Benes (Czechoslovakia)
1949-1950	Gerard Spelberg (Netherlands)
1950-1952	Ronald McGraw (Great Britain)
1952-1954	Kurt Jenney (Switzerland)
1954-1956	Carel Delbeek (Netherlands)
1956-1958	Axel Hoffer (USA)
1958-1959	Donald Dunkley (Great Britain)
1959-1961	Grenville Needham (Great Britain)
1961-1962	Spencer Lavan (USA)
1962-1964	Banz Probst (Switzerland)
1964-1965	Martin Fieldhouse (Great Britain)
1965-1967	Helmut Manteuffel (Federal Republic of Germany)
1967-1969	Andrew Patrick (Great Britain)
1969-1971	Paul Reiber (USA)
1971-1973	Geoff Blanc (France)
1973-1975	Lucie Meijer (Netherlands)
1975-1976	Wayne Arnason (Canada)
1976-1978	Christine Hayhurst (Great Britain)
1978-1980	Renate Bauer (FR Germany)

Acknowledgments

The Unitarian Sunday School Society has been a financial supporter of both the original *Follow the Gleam* manuscript and the current, updated edition, *We Would Be One*—offering grants at crucial times of early project development when no financial resources or publishing commitment had been secured. Our deep thanks to them.

We would also like to thank Mary Benard and the staff at Skinner House for their support and guidance in the creation of the revised edition. Special thanks also goes to Hillevi M. Wyman for typing the complete original and to Frances O'Donnell, curator of manuscripts and archives at Andover-Harvard Theological Library, for helping us find photographs from the original edition.

From Wayne Arnason:

This book's precursor, *Follow the Gleam*, would have remained only a personal project if not for the encouragement and tireless support of the late Rev. Carl Seaburg, who served as the UUA's Information Officer from 1971 to 1985. Carl is best remembered for his important liturgical reference books, *Great Occasions* and *Celebrating Christmas*. He was a lifelong Universalist who was president of the Universalist Youth fellowship from 1948 to 1949, so he had a personal interest in this history. In the days before Skinner House, he also encouraged many authors with tips on pursuing publication. Carl took it upon himself to be my editor and suggested that everything about my project could be better than it was. As the idea of Skinner House Books was coming into being, he encouraged me to submit the manuscript for consideration as a "Skinner House Monograph." The personal interlude memoirs between chapters were his idea. He did much of the fund-raising to support the printing costs himself. I owe Carl Seaburg a deep debt of gratitude and remember him fondly.

The manuscript benefited from the assistance of the following people:

- Alan Seaburg of Harvard Divinity School and Kate Hitchings of the Universalist Historical Library at Tufts assisted with my research.
- The Continental Youth-Adult Committee of 1979 offered a generous grant.
- Eugene Navias, the late Starr Williams, Eugene Pickett, Robert Senghas, Robert Nelson West, and Leon Hopper read early versions of the manuscript and offered valuable suggestions.
- David Parke offered a thorough critique of the manuscript and assisted with fund-raising.
- Dr. Conrad Wright supervised the writing of the final draft at Harvard Divinity School in 1976.
- Numerous youth group veterans were more than generous with their time in writing memoirs, providing photographs, and answering questions. Besides those whose memoirs have been printed in the text, I wish to acknowledge important conversations with Dick Kuch, Alice Harrison, Dana Maclean Greeley, Richard Woodman, Peter Baldwin, Deither Gehrmann, Leon Hopper, Charles Eddis, Christopher Raible, Peter Raible, and Richard Kossow.
- So much of the energy and enthusiasm for undertaking this revised manuscript has come from Rebecca Scott. She has been a joy to work with.

From Rebecca Scott:

I remember reading the original edition of *Follow the Gleam* when I was a youth involved in YRUU. More recently, I discovered that, since it was out of print, I was one of a dwindling number of people who were aware of this interesting and important aspect of our Unitarian and Universalist history. With an interest in seeing this history made available to the general public, I approached Wayne Arnason to see if he would be interested in doing a revised edition, and I have been very honored and pleased to be his partner on the project.

I would also like to thank the following people who agreed to be interviewed and contributed their memories and experiences to the Common Ground and YRUU chapters of the book: Caprice Young, Kathryn Deal, Ellen Brandenburg, Scott Keeler, Anne King, Jennifer Martin, Paula Nett, Jason Happel, Parisa Parsa, David Levine, Jesse Jaeger, Abbey Tennis, Jacob Larsen, Julie-Ann Silberman-Bunn, Ben Ford, Dave Williams, Joseph Lyons, Sarah Gibb, Hank Peirce, Lisa Feldstein, Rob Keithan, Eugene Pickett, David Provost, Bruce Southworth, Graham Smith, Julie Rising, Sean Ramsey, Meg Riley, Coleen Murphy, Kevin Appleton, and Jory Agate.

Notes

Laying the Foundations

p. 2 ...*and social-service and reform work.* C. H. Lyttle, *Freedom Moves West* (Boston: Beacon Press, 1952), p. 230.

p. 2 ...*Thirty groups known as "Unity Clubs."* President William Howard Taft became active in the Unity Club in his home church, in Cincinnati, Ohio, after graduating from Yale. He later recalled that ambition to be president of the United States began with his election to the presidency of that club.

p. 2 ...*organized a highly successful YPSCE group.* The Bay City, Michigan, church has since been dissolved.

p. 3 ...*would teach young people cant and hypocrisy.* Carl Henry and Herbert Briggs (ed.), "A Historical Souvenir of the YPCU" (1893). Brochure located in the Universalist Historical Library at the Andover Harvard Library, Cambridge, Massachusetts (UHL).

p. 5 ...*the ideals of worship, service, and truth.* Van Ness had been the AUA's Pacific Coast mission secretary from 1889-1893, and was at that time minister of the Second Church in Boston. He had the opportunity to see the different young people's groups on both coasts.

p. 7 ...*sparked the group's decision to enter the missionary field.* Nash became dean of Lombard College. Shinn was the most celebrated of the Universalist missionaries. He was responsible for the creation of many churches. Ferry Beach was founded in 1901 out of the regular summer meetings Shinn conducted at The Weirs, New Hampshire, and later at Saco, Maine.

p. 7 ...*and the thing was done.* Henry and Briggs, op. cit., pp. 11-12.

p. 8 ...*two cents a week for a year!* Quoted in Harry Adams Hersey, "A Brief History of the YPCU" in *The Christian Leader,* July 8, 1939 (Boston: Universalist Publishing House).

p. 8 ...*Shinn Memorial Church in Chattanooga, Tennessee.* The church had a memorial stained glass window to Nash as well.

p. 10 ...*amended to allow such membership.* Quoted in F.B. Morris, "The Young

People's Christian Union of Massachusetts and Rhode Island: A Complete History 1889-1939," p. 7 (UHL).

p. 11 ...*such memberships had begun to die out.* The provision for life membership would remain in the YPRU, AUY, and LRY constitutions, however. Honorary life membership recipients were to include Peter Baldwin upon his resignation as LRY executive director in 1966, Dana Greeley, upon his retirement from the UUA presidency in 1969, and Carl Seaburg, cited in 1978 a friend to many LRY executive committees.

p. 12 ...*sought to keep clear of entangling alliances.* Clinton Lee Scott, *The Universalist Church of America: A Short History* (Boston: Universalist Historical Society: 1957) p. 69.

p. 13 ...*but the Board overcame all such difficulties.* F.B. Morris, op. cit., p. 12.

p. 13 ...*however proper and fruitful.* Hersey, op. cit., p. 697.

Building the Institution

p. 19 ...*first woman president of the YPCU.* The Unitarians did not elect a woman as president until 1945.

p. 20 ...*was still very New England-oriented.* Somewhat more than half of these actually affiliated and paid dues to the YPRU, however.

p. 20 ...*the absence of any other representatives.* Raible would go on to a distinguished career culminating in his ministry to First Unitarian Church in Dallas, Texas.

p. 20 ...*too old to be president of YPRU.* Robert Raible, in personal correspondence to Christopher Raible, 1956. Charles Bolster and Ed Furber were presidents in 1926-1928 and 1924-1926, respectively.

p. 24 ..."*the epoch of youth only" was beginning.* Hersey, op. cit., p. 646.

p. 26 ...*in order to sleep outside.* Personal interview with Dana Greeley, January 28, 1976.

p. 26 ...*ultimately the whole denomination.* Hersey, op. cit., p. 650.

p. 27 ...*when the Student Federation of Religious Liberals (SFRL) was created.* I am indebted to Christopher Raible for access to personal correspondence from his father, Robert Raible, concerning his experiences in SFRL.

Cooperation at Home and Abroad

p. 33 ...*implications of a merger.* Personal interview with Dana Greeley, January 28, 1976.

p. 33 ...*establishing a "Free Church of America."* Report of the YPRU Committee on Interdenominational Relations, 1933. From the YPRU files, Unitarian Universalist Association archives.

p. 34 ...*action was "postponed" until another year.* Scott, op. cit., p. 70.

p. 36 ...*take our minds off peace for a bit.* From the YPRU files on the Peace Caravans. (UHL)

p. 37 ...*the light that shall bring the dawn*. Thanks to Gene Navias for telling us that "Follow the Gleam" was not Universalist in origin. The song is copyrighted by the Young Women's Christian Association of America, and was the Silver Bay Contest winner song at Bryn Mawr College.

p. 37 ...*We pledge to the life of the world*. The words to the YPRU hymn were written by Sara Cumins, the executive secretary of the YPRU during the mid 1920s.

p. 38 ...*group programs from the 1920s are offered below*. These topics were chosen from a YPCU group's program notes not only for their exemplary nature but for the titles themselves.

p. 39 ...*experiences in the Rhode Island Insane Asylum*. Quoted in Benjamin Zablocki, *The Joyful Community* (Baltimore: Penguin Books: 1971), p. 66-67.

pp. 40 ...*describing the atmosphere of the time*. For these and other facts related to the early history of the free religious youth groups of Germany we are indebted to research undertaken by Deither Gehrmann printed as a monograph for the information of IRF members in 1953.

Organization and Readjustment

p. 46 ...*drastically alter the shape of the Unitarian movement*. For a complete summary of the content and consequences of the Commission of Appraisal report, see the essay by Carol R. Morris, "It Was Noontime Here" in C.C. Wright (ed.), *A Stream of Light* (Boston: Unitarian Universalist Association: 1975).

p. 52 ...*the group elected Dana Klotzle president and Raymond Hopkins vice president*. Klotzle would go on into parish ministry, and serve as the Unitarian Universalist Association's representative at the United Nations until the time of his death in 1974. Hopkins would become first vice president of UUA.

Internationalism and the Cold War

p. 63 ...*the communist cell to which he himself had belonged*. See Ralph Lord Roy, *Communism and the Churches* (New York: Harcourt and Brace: 1960).

p. 64 ...*led by communist sympathizers*. Drawn from research by Rev. Philip Zwerling for his unpublished manuscript, "The Fritchman Case" (1974).

p. 64 ...*things she wanted to do*. Ibid.

p. 66 ...*be "only nominally affiliated."* Quoted in Roy, op. cit., p. 466.

p. 67 ...*Fritchman left 25 Beacon Street*. Zwerling, op. cit. and *The Christian Register* various issues, 1945-1947. Valuable personal accounts of these years and events are found in S. Fritchman, *Heretic* (Skinner House: Boston 1977) pp. 47-101.

p. 68 ...*and other democratic countries*. From a copy of the telegram in the private papers of David Parke.

We Would Be One

p. 79 ...*because of lack of information. Unitarian Unite!* report of the Commission on Planning and Review: October 15, 1947.

p. 80 ...*of secretarial staff under him. The Christian Register*, Vol. 129, No. 2 (February 1950).

p. 89 ...*to hold their 1951 conferences and annual meetings together.* The 1948 AUY Convention was held at Lake Couchiching, Ontario, Canada. Eddis was a Canadian, and at this conference held on Canadian soil, it was finally formally acknowledged that the AUY would be referred to as a "continental" rather than "national" organization.

p. 92 ...*setting the stage for the final vote.* In this regard, we note a resolution passed by the AUY Council at its 1952 meetings, entitled "Repeal of Terrestrial Law": "Moved: (L. Hopper) Whereas it is clearly evident that a 24 hour day is not sufficient to conduct our business, therefore be it resolved, that at following conventions AUY operate on a 40 hour day. Duly seconded and passed with Rising Acclamation."

p. 93 ...*associate director for college activities* (i.e., *the Channing-Murray Foundation*). Eileen Layton, having been the AUY president for 1952-1953, functioned virtually as associate director of LRY during that time. AUY hired her officially in mid 1952.

p. 93 ...*independence became even stronger.* Leon Hopper, "A Short Subjective History of the Unitarian and Universalist Youth Movements" (AUY Files: 1963), p. 4.

LRY Comes of Age

p. 98 ...*the manner in which they had been performing them.* Personal interview with Alice Harrison, October 7, 1975.

p. 99 ...*I have nothing to say.* Ibid.

p. 102 ...*preserve its unique organization.* From Bill Gold's "Some observations on the basis of fifteen months as Executive Director of LRY," UUA Archives, Boston.

p. 105 ...*elected second vice president of IRF.* Kurt Jenny was the president of that executive committee, and Christopher Raible served as corresponding secretary.

p. 108 ...*was elected LRY president.* Lavan would go on to become IRF president as well.

p. 113 ...*sophomore year in college, but not beyond.* The youth program conducted by the Church of the Larger Fellowship should be noted at this point. CLF was founded in 1951 to provide services to isolated religious liberals. By the 1960s, it published religious education material for its Junior Fellowship (age 6–11), Uniteens (age 12–14), Junior Fellowship Youth (JFY, age 15–18), and Young Adults (age 18–college age). JFY and Young Adults affiliated with LRY and the Channing-Murray program, but by 1968 LRY had lost touch with them.

The Youth Agenda

p. 129 ...*an exceedingly efficient super-organization*. Peter Baldwin, "Final Report" to Liberal Religious Youth, 1966.

p. 132 ...*all a part of the challenge*. Fritz West, "L.R.Y.: Fact and Vision," 1966.

p. 133 ...*before the lid blew off the culture*. Baldwin, op cit.

p. 134 ...*bailed out several SRL members*. Homer Jack, quoted in Student Religious Liberals newsletter, 1964.

The New Community

p. 161 ...*the committee should include alternatives*. Quoted in Special Committee on Youth Programs report to Unitarian Universalist Association Board of Trustees, November 1977. Full text available at www.lryer.org/uuyouthhistory/scoyp.

p. 164 ...*staff support that other activities receive*. Ibid.

Looking for Common Ground

p. 169 ...*couldn't provide the necessary programs*. Personal interview with Eugene Pickett, July 19, 2004

p. 169 ...*that everyone will support*. "The Dozen Most Frequently Asked Questions about Common Ground," Unitarian Universalist Association Youth Office document, around 1980.

p. 170 ...*any change would signal the end*. Personal interview with Dave Williams, January 30, 2003.

p. 171 ...*She was someone I trusted*. Personal interview with Wayne Arnason, 2003.

p. 171 ...*concerned with youth programming*. "The Dozen Most Frequently Asked Questions," op cit.

p. 171 ...*gathering a delegation together*. Arnason, op cit.

p. 172 ...*excellent shared leadership as well*. Personal interview with Lisa Feldstein, May 30, 2003.

p. 172 ...*Was this organization just for teenagers?* Personal interview with Laila Ibrahim, February 8, 2003.

p. 173 ...*I wouldn't have been eligible for anything in LRY?* Williams, op cit.

p.173 ...*I'm losing everything*. Jan Eller-Issacs, comment at Unitarian Universalist Association General Assembly workshop, "Youth Leadership: Our Legacy, Our Future," June 27, 2003.

p. 174 ... *communication between youth and adults*. The Statement of Purpose and the goals cited were written and adopted by the delegates to Common Ground Youth Assembly, August 9-15, 1981, at Carleton College in Northfield, Minnesota.

p. 174 ...*was to be a service organization*. Arnason, op cit.

p. 174 ...*You will hear from us, I promise you.* Oren Peterson, "Common Ground —a precursor?" Unitarian Universalist World, October 15, 1981.

p. 175 ...*the difficult task we set out to do.* Personal interview with Anne Heller, 2003.

p. 175 ...*the one who betrayed LRY.* Comment by Julie-Anne Silberman-Bunn at Unitarian Universalist Association General Assembly workshop, "Youth Leadership: Our Legacy, Our Future," June 27, 2003.

p. 175 ...*Board representation for youth?* Wayne Arnason, letter to Common Ground participants, October 1, 1981.

p. 176 ...*was partially a budgetary concern.* Pickett, op cit.

p. 176 ...*for youth programming and a youth Trustee.* Youth-Adult Committee and Youth Programming Committee of the Saint Lawrence District, letter to Eugene Pickett and the UUA Board of Trustees, January 23, 1982.

p. 176 ...*a precedent of rule-making that confirms that perception.* Vonnie Hicks, letter to "Common Ground Communicants and friends of youth programming," January 15, 1982.

p. 177 ...*their own standards on room assignments.* Youth Assembly Planning Committee, "Common Ground report to Unitarian Universalist Association Board of Trustees," 1982.

p. 177 ...*was all-consuming and exhausting.* Feldstein, op cit.

p. 177...*our doings in order to further the community?* Youth Assembly Planning Committee, op cit.

p. 178 ...*consensus about these issues among themselves.* Youth Assembly Planning Committee, op cit.

p. 178 ...*clear rules of behavior prohibiting sex.* Resolution passed by the Board of Directors of the Central Midwest District of the UUA on September 19, 1981, at their meeting in Racine, Wisconsin.

p. 179 ...*it must be met with some firmness.* Frank Schulman, letter to Wayne Arnason, August 24, 1981.

p. 179 ...*including sexual affection.* Resolution passed by the Pacific Central District chapter of the Unitarian Universalist Minister's Association on January 20, 1982.

p. 179 ...*too much time-consuming clarification.* Margaret McKee, secretary to the Southwest delegation to Common Ground, in the "Southwest District Delegation Common Ground Report," 1981.

p. 179 ...*irritated with the discussion because of the time it took from the main discussions.* Schulman, op cit.

p. 180 ...*older, hippie advisors who had been involved in LRY.* Personal interview with Hank Pierce, 2003.

p. 181 ...*we had no real say in what was happening.* Personal interview with David Levine, August 5, 2004.

p. 182 ...*You can tell them I said that.* Pierce, op cit.

p. 182 ...*we were all really excited about it.* Levine, op cit.

p. 182 ...*people had hurt themselves.* Participant feedback form from Common Ground II, 1982.

p. 183 ...*(forgive the word, please).* Andrea Dawson, feedback form from Common Ground II, 1982.

p. 183 ...*so many people in so little time,* participant feedback form from Common Ground II, 1982.

p. 183 ...*life would always be like it was at Common Ground.* Levine, op cit.

Starting Over

p. 234 ...*the second largest generational group, behind only their parents.* David K. Foot, *Boom, Bust and Echo.* (Toronto: Macfarlane Walter and Ross, 1996).

Paths in the Jungle

p. 213 ...*as intellectual, moral, sentient, aesthetic, and mortal beings.* Hugo Hollereth, *Relating to Our World* (Boston: Beacon Press: 1974), p. 38.

Index